GOD'S
ARMORBEARER
1 & 2

THE DAILY
JOURNEY

TERRY NANCE

DESTINY IMAGE® PUBLISHERS, INC.

P.O. Box 310, Shippensburg, PA 17257-0310

"Speaking to the Purposes of God for This Generation and for the Generations to Come."

This book and all other Destiny Image, Revival Press, Mercy Place, Fresh Bread, Destiny Image Fiction, and Treasure House books are available at Christian bookstores and distributors worldwide.

For a U.S. bookstore nearest you, call 1-800-722-6774.

For more information on foreign distributors, call 717-532-3040.

Or reach us on the Internet: www.destinyimage.com

ISBN 10: 0-7684-3145-X   ISBN 13: 978-0-7684-3145-2

Previously published as: Developing a Spirit of Excellence in Serving God's Leaders by Harrison House copyright© 2004.

Previous ISBN: 978-1-57794-639-7 and 1-57794-639-1

For Worldwide Distribution, Printed in the U.S.A.

1 2 3 4 5 6 7 8 9 10 11 / 13 12 11 10 09

TABLE OF CONTENTS

INTRODUCTION

One evening back in 1983, I felt a prompting to get alone with the Lord. I went into our living room and began to pray, when suddenly I was quickened in my spirit to read the story of David and Saul. I knew the Lord was ready to reveal something to me. As I began to read, I came to First Samuel 16:21:

> And David came to Saul, and stood before him: and he loved him greatly; and he became his armorbearer.

Suddenly the Lord quickened the word "armorbearer" to me. He said, *I have called you to be your pastor's "armorbearer."* He was referring to Pastor Happy Caldwell of Agape Church in Little Rock, Arkansas, whom I served as an armorbearer for 23 years.

What does an armorbearer do? In Old Testament days, he had the awesome responsibility of carrying his master's shield into battle and keeping him safe. Today, God's armorbearers are God-called ministers, chosen and sent by the Spirit of God to assist leadership with the vision He has placed within them. These ministers may include those who are part of the paid staff of churches and ministries as well as those believers who volunteer in the ministry of helps for their local church. These armorbearers take the load off the leadership and help to impart the leader's vision to the people. They are intensely loyal, faithful, and service-motivated people whose duties may include serving as bodyguard, friend, companion, confidant, and spiritual warrior, as well as an interminable list of other services. The position of the armorbearer is one that requires great love, honor, tolerance, and watchfulness. But being an armorbearer is not just an office; it is also the attitude and the heart of a servant. The greatest in God's Kingdom will be the servant of all.

The True Spirit of an Armorbearer

At the time in my life when God gave me the revelation of being an armorbearer, He was helping me to get my priorities in order. It is my prayer that as you study these devotions each day, He will do the same for you. We live in a world that seems to know very little about laying down one's life for another. Instead of offering ourselves to wait on others, we in the Church often expect spiritual leaders to wait on us. A full understanding of this concept of servanthood is vital to the Christian, however, especially if he knows he has been called into the ministry.

One of the most profound relationships of an armorbearer serving the man of God is that of Elisha serving Elijah. It is clear that you and I will never flow in the anointing of Elisha until we have learned to serve an Elijah. Jesus put it this way: *"Greater love hath no man than this, that a man*

lay down his life for his friends" (John 15:13). It is not difficult to claim that we are submitted to Jesus, but the question is, are we submitted to another human being? That is a different story.

A Note to Qualify the Point

Because of abuses of power and the mistakes of some misguided leaders, submission has often gotten a bad rap. This doesn't, however, negate the biblical principle or the need for a godly chain of command. Under no circumstances would God call you to submit to a leader who would manipulate you, control you, or abuse you in any way. The leader must be someone who can be trusted. His manner of life and track record in ministry must have produced good fruit. His character must be solid. On the other hand, the armorbearer must be sure that he has heard from the Holy Spirit and that God is indeed calling him to serve this particular leader.

That being said, this devotional is written with the assumption that the leader you serve is not abusing his power but is operating within the principles set forth in the Bible. If the line has become blurred for you and you are concerned that your relationship with your leader has become unhealthy, perhaps it would be a good idea to seek godly counsel outside of your local body.

Abuse of power happens, but so does the God-ordained working relationship between leader and armorbearer. We don't want to throw out the baby with the bathwater, so to speak. In fact, I believe God has prepared an armorbearer for every leader called to the fivefold ministry. And that is the purpose of this book—to assist you in developing your full potential as a God-appointed armorbearer.

The Need for Armorbearers

There are many reasons why armorbearers are needed, but one is that I see so many great ministries that are built around one person. What will happen when the leader is out of town? It is of no credit to a pastor, or any man of God, to know that unless he is present physically, the sheep cannot function. The sheep should have their eyes fixed on Jesus, not the leader. And there should be capable men to run the ministry while the leader is absent.

Where would we be today if Jesus had not put a portion of Himself into the 12 disciples? What would have happened if, on the day He ascended to the Father, there had been no one there to see Him go and then to take up His ministry on earth?

I ask every pastor and spiritual leader this vital question: If you were taken off the scene today, where would your ministry be tomorrow? Most would have to admit that it would suffer. Jesus' ministry increased and multiplied. That's because there were armorbearers standing with Him.

Armorbearer **Defined**

The word *armorbearer* is listed 18 times in Strong's con-cordance, all references being found in the Old Testament. Each is referenced by two numbers, indicating that the word was originally translated from two Hebrew words. The term's original meaning must be firmly established if the true idea is to be fully understood.

As noted, the *King James* word "armorbearer" was trans-lated from two Hebrew words. The first is *nasa* or *nacah (naw-saw')*. This is a primary word meaning "to *lift.*"[1] It has a great variety of applications, both figuratively and literally. Some of the more interesting applications are to: accept, advance, bear, bear up, carry away, cast, desire, furnish, fur-ther, give, help, hold up, lift, pardon, raise, regard, respect, stir up, yield.

The second Hebrew word is *keliy (kel-ee')*, which comes from the root word *kalah (kaw-law')*, meaning "to *end.*"[2] Some of the applications of this root word are to: complete, consume, destroy utterly, be done, finish, fulfill, long, bring to pass, wholly reap, make clean riddance.

We can see that the duty of the armorbearer was to stand beside his leader to assist him, to lift him up, and to protect him against any enemy that might attack him. The same is true today. The New Testament armorbearer is called to stand beside his leader to assist him, advance him, bear him up, help him, lift him, regard and respect him, stir him up, yield to him, and protect him. It is an awesome privilege and responsibility indeed.

Your Role

Pastors, others in full-time ministry, and all spiritual leaders need and benefit greatly from armorbearers who are called alongside to help them. Whether one serves as a parking-lot attendant, an usher, a Sunday school teacher, or an associate pastor, the role of the armorbearer is vital to the success of the minister under whom he or she serves. No ministry is a one-man show; it takes a team effort.

To the person in the fivefold ministry, I say this: You will never arrive at a place where you do not have to submit to anyone. The spirit of an armorbearer is the spirit of Christ. It is the heart of a servant. In that way, every believer serves as an armorbearer in some capacity.

The purpose of this devotional book is to give you a revelation of the *spirit of an armorbearer* in regard to your relationship with the man or woman of God in your life. It is also designed to encourage, challenge, instruct, and nurture armorbearers on a daily basis. These devotions may be used by individual readers, or they may serve as the centerpiece of a Bible study or a course for those who serve. As you seek to fulfill God's call on your life, it is my prayer that you will grow in the knowledge of, and experience for yourself, what it means to be *God's armorbearer.*

Editor's note: For simplicity's sake, armorbearers, as well as the leaders whom they serve, are referred to in the male gender throughout the text. However, we recognize that the Bible clearly reveals that men and women alike may be called to serve in both capacities. *"There is neither Jew nor Greek, there is neither bond nor free, there is neither male nor female: for ye are all one in Christ Jesus"* (Gal. 3:28).

In addition, the term *leader* is used to represent the man or woman of God whom the armorbearer is called to serve. *Leader* refers to:

- pastors,
- heads of ministries,
- those called to the fivefold ministry,
- spiritual leaders in any capacity, and
- those in authority in the Body of Christ.

Endnotes

1. James Strong, "Hebrew and Chaldee Dictionary," in Strong's Exhaustive Concordance of the Bible (Nashville: Abingdon, 1890) entry #5423, s.v. "nasa."

2. Strong, "Hebrew Dictionary," entry #3627, s.v. "keliy."

MAINTAINING RIGHT ATTITUDES

Now your attitudes and thoughts must all be constantly changing for the better. Yes, you must be a new and different person, holy and good. Clothe yourself with this new nature (Ephesians 4:23-24 TLB)

The Bible states that *"many are called, but few are chosen"* (Matt. 22:14). Becoming the chosen of God is a choice on your part to pray and to live in faith, integrity, diligence, and excellence of ministry. You must determine to have those attributes in your life and to be committed to the will of God, no matter the cost.

Having and maintaining right attitudes is crucial if one is to be a true armorbearer. Allow the Holy Spirit to reveal the attitudes present in your heart. Ask Him to show you if you have failed to flow with your spiritual leaders. If you have, then make a quality decision to rid yourself of any trace of rebellion, strife, contention, competitiveness, and unforgiveness, and determine to faithfully fulfill your rightful place in the Body of Christ.

The enemy seeks to divide and conquer. He knows that *"where envying and strife is, there is confusion and every evil work"* (James 3:16). It is impossible for the spiritual leader's church or ministry to reach its full potential if these attitudes are present in those he leads, especially if they are present in the one called to support him as armorbearer.

Choose today to rid yourself of any ungodly attitudes, and in their place, adopt those attitudes that are holy and good. Clothe yourself with the new nature.

Developing the Spirit of an Armorbearer

- Recognize that the enemy is out to destroy the ministry that you are called to support.

- Refuse to be used by the enemy by confessing any wrong attitudes you have toward your leader or his ministry and receive forgiveness.

- Meditate on James 3:13–18 (NIV) and commit to walk in the wisdom of God that is pure, peaceable, full of good fruits, impartial, and without hypocrisy: *"Who is a wise man and endued with knowledge among you? Let him show out of a good conversation his works with meekness of wisdom. But if ye have bitter envying and strife in your hearts, glory not, and lie not against the truth. This wisdom descendeth not from above, but is earthly, sensual, devilish. For where envying and strife is, there is confusion and every evil work.*

But the wisdom that is from above is first pure, then peaceable, gentle, and easy to be entreated, full of mercy and good fruits, without partiality, and without hypocrisy. And the fruit of righteousness is sown in peace of them that make peace."

Heavenly Father, You know the condition of my heart even better than I know it myself. Reveal any wrong attitudes, such as rebellion, envy, strife, contention, competitiveness, or unforgiveness. As I confess them to You, thank You that Your blood cleanses me from all unrighteousness. Today I commit to walk in the new nature You have given me, which is full of wisdom and good fruit. Amen.

THE DUTIES OF
AN ARMORBEARER

PROVIDING STRENGTH
FOR HIS LEADER

[Epaphroditus] is a true brother, a faithful worker, and a courageous soldier. And he was your messenger to help me [Paul] in my need (Philippians 2:25 NLT).

One of the first duties of an armorbearer is to be a source of strength for his leader. To do this, the armorbearer must stay built up in his spirit and be strong in the Lord himself. As a result of this inner strength, the armorbearer's very presence will display and produce an attitude of faith and peace.

If you are to be successful in service as an armorbearer to your leader, he must sense the joy and victory that is an integral part of your lifestyle. That in itself will minister to him. It is a great relief to the spiritual leader to know that he does not have to carry his assistant physically, mentally, and spiritually. Many times I have seen pastors drained physically and emotionally because their associates were always in need of something. Your leader has plenty of sheep to take care of; he doesn't need another.

This is not to say that you do not have needs or that the leader you serve will never minister to you. Certainly, like all believers, you have needs, and more than likely the ministry of your leader is one you receive spiritual nourishment from. But as far as your relationship and interaction with your leader are concerned, your first goal as armorbearer should be to assist him, giving him much-needed rest in mind and body. You do this by demonstrating that your faith is strong and active. Ultimately, this must come from your own personal relationship with God.

Developing the Spirit of an Armorbearer

Some things you can do to stay strong in the Lord include:

- staying full of God's Word (Prov. 4:20-22);

- building yourself up on your most holy faith by praying in the Holy Ghost (Jude 1:20);

- drawing on the joy of the Lord for your strength (Neh. 8:10);

- being strengthened by might by God's Spirit in your inner man (Eph. 3:16); and

- maintaining a personal and intimate relationship with God (Rev. 3:20).

Dear God, I am committed to be a source of strength to the one I serve and to contribute to his well-being. When

I am going through challenges and feel anything but strong, remind me to draw my strength and direction from You. I purpose to pull on You, the all-sufficient One, not on the man You've called me to serve. Amen.

RESPECT, ACCEPTANCE,
& TOLERANCE

Obey your leaders and submit to their authority. They keep watch over you as men who must give an account. Obey them so that their work will be a joy, not a burden, for that would be of no advantage to you (Hebrews 13:17 NIV)

An armorbearer must have a deep-down sense of respect for his leader and acceptance for and tolerance of his leader's personality and way of doing things. God made us all different. Many times, your pastor's way of doing things will differ from yours. That difference should not be allowed to cause a problem for you or your spiritual leader, however.

Several years ago, I learned a secret that has helped me to flow in harmony with my pastor. I determined that if the end result of my pastor's plan is to build and extend the Kingdom of God and win souls for Jesus, then I am willing to flow with the plan. Our goal is the same; our methods may be different. But what does it really matter whose methods are used, as long as the goal is reached?

If you will adopt this attitude toward your pastor, there will be a knitting of hearts between the two of you. He will know that you are not there to argue with him or to challenge his decisions, but that you are there to work with him in achieving his God-given objectives.

Developing the Spirit of an Armorbearer

Examine your heart by asking yourself the following questions:

- Has God called me to serve this leader?

- What is the leader's goal? Is it the same as mine?

- If our goal is the same, how do our methods for achieving it differ?

- Are the leader's methods in line with God's Word?

- Have I prayed for my leader to be led by the Spirit in this endeavor?

- What is my attitude toward my leader and his way of doing things?

- Where do I need to adjust my attitude? Am I willing to adopt my leader's methods? If not, why?

- Assuming that you share your leader's goals, that his methods line up with God's Word, and that you are willing to adopt his methods, make the quality decision today to submit to your leader's direction and follow him cheerfully and wholeheartedly.

Heavenly Father, sometimes it is hard to "go with the flow" because my leader does things so differently from the way I would do them. I acknowledge, however, that You are the One who put him into this place of authority and You've called me to assist him. As long as his methods don't contradict Your Word, I will submit myself to them. I pray continually that my leader will hear Your voice and obey Your commands. Amen.

UNDERSTANDING THE
LEADER'S THOUGHTS

Fulfill ye my joy, that ye be likeminded, having the same love, being of one accord, of one mind (Philippians 2:2).

An armorbearer must instinctively understand his leader's thoughts. I can hear what you are probably thinking right now: *My leader and I just don't think alike.* That should come as no surprise; no two people think alike on everything. And that is one of the problems that must be dealt with in being an armorbearer to another.

Instead of complaining about your differences, begin to discover and confess your agreement: "In Jesus' name, I understand how my leader thinks, and I flow with him in the spirit of understanding."

Remember, the disciples were with Jesus for three long years; yet they did not begin to think as He thought until after He had died, was buried and resurrected, ascended into Heaven, and sent the Holy Ghost. Just as God's Spirit was eventually imparted to these men, after a period of time, your leader's spirit will come upon you and the two of you will become likeminded.

In the meantime, you can choose to be of one mind and one accord with your leader. In Second Corinthians 13:11, the apostle Paul instructs us to be of one mind. Peter echoes this admonition in First Peter 3:8. From these verses it is clear that being of one mind is something we can determine to do. It begins with a decision, but over time, as you put this into practice, your thoughts will become one with your leader.

Developing the Spirit of an Armorbearer

- If you've been griping and complaining, stop!

- Determine the things you and your leader agree on.

- Ask God to give you understanding and insight into how your leader thinks, and why. Understand his personality, temperament, and background.

- Respect the fact that even if you don't understand the way your leader thinks about a matter, he has been put into his position by God.

- Trust that your leader's thoughts and motives are pure, knowing that he is accountable to God.

- Pray for your leader and trust that God is at work in his life.

• Determine to be likeminded with your leader.

Dear God, I don't always understand how my leader thinks or why he thinks the way he does. Sometimes I just don't agree with him. I confess my sin of complaining and ask You to give me wisdom and insight into my leader. He is first and foremost Your child, so I trust You to lead and guide him. Help me to see where we do agree, and give me the grace to go forward from there. I choose to be of one mind and one accord with my leader, and I thank You for blessing our unity. Amen.

WALKING IN AGREEMENT
& SUBMISSION

Servants, be obedient to them that are your masters according to the flesh, with fear and trembling, in singleness of your heart, as unto Christ; not with eyeservice, as menpleasers; but as the servants of Christ, doing the will of God from the heart; with good will doing service, as to the Lord, and not to men (Ephesians 6:5-7).

The armorbearer must walk in agreement with, and submission to, his leader. In order to be an armorbearer, you must have it settled in your heart that according to Romans 13:1-2, all authority is ordained of God. You must make up your mind to submit to your leader in the same way that you submit to Jesus.

The apostle Peter tells us, *"Likewise, ye younger, submit yourselves unto the elders"* (1 Pet. 5:5). Notice that there are no conditions to this command. The exception would if an elder or leader were to give instructions that violate the Scriptures. Then, of course, the armorbearer is to obey the higher authority of God's Word. God would never violate His Word. For our purpose here, we will assume that your leader is operating in line with the Bible.

Most Christians do not understand the true meaning of submission to authority. The Bible teaches that all authority has been instituted by God Himself, so to refuse to submit to God's delegated authority is to refuse to submit to God.

"Oh, but I will always submit myself to God!"

This is a comment I hear quite often. But how can a person claim to be submitted to God if he or she refuses to submit to God's delegated authority?

Many armorbearers declare that they are submitted to their leader, but they really don't have revelation of submission until they learn to submit when they disagree with their leader. This is where they find out what is in their heart; this is the test of true submission. Can you submit when you disagree with your leader's decision?

We must not look at the person but at the office he occupies. We do not regard the man but the position. We obey not the individual himself but God's authority in him (which will always line up with His Word). Anything less than full submission is rebellion, and rebellion is the principle on which satan and his kingdom operate.

It is sad to think that we Christians can preach the truth with our lips but go right on living by a satanic principle in our everyday lives. How can we expect to preach the Gospel to others and bring them under God's authority if we ourselves have not yet fully submitted to that authority?

There is a spirit of independence at large in the Body of Christ today. Independent churches produce independent spirits. We must break this spirit and begin to rightly discern the whole Body of Christ.

Always remember this: God will never establish you as an authority until you have first learned to submit to authority.

Developing the Spirit of an Armorbearer

- Study and meditate on Romans 13:1-2: *"Everyone must submit himself to the governing authorities, for there is no authority except that which God has established. The authorities that exist have been established by God. Consequently, he who rebels against the authority is rebelling against what God has instituted, and those who do so will bring judgment on themselves."*

- Assuming that your leader submits to God's Word, renew your commitment to submit to his spiritual oversight. As you submit to him, in reality you are submitting yourself to God. Both you and your leader will be blessed, and the Gospel will be advanced.

Heavenly Father, I see from Your Word how important it is for me to submit to my leader as I submit to Christ.

I believe You have placed him in the position of authority, and I am committed to obey Your Word by submitting to that authority. I thank You for giving my leader the mind of Christ. I pray that He will always obey Your Word and direction and that the Kingdom of God will be advanced. Amen.

ADVANCING HIS LEADER'S
DREAMS & DESIRES

Look not every man on his own things, but every man also on the things of others. Let this mind be in you, which was also in Christ Jesus: who...made himself of no reputation, and took upon him the form of a servant (Philippians 2:4-7).

When a person serves as an armorbearer, he lays aside his personal desires to help fulfill the desires of the leader he serves. One day, while I was serving Pastor Caldwell, I asked God, "What about *my* dreams and desires?" He told me to give them to Him and to work at fulfilling the desires and visions of my pastor. He assured me that if I would do that, He would see to it that my dreams and desires would be fulfilled. He reminded me that Jesus did exactly this same thing when He gave up His own will and desires in order to do the Father's will for His life. In turn, the Father made sure that Jesus' dreams and visions were all fulfilled.

I can honestly say that God has done that very thing in my life. In 1977, I had a vision to reach out and go into many nations. In 1982, I began to see that vision come to pass. I have already traveled to over 40 countries and have preached in most of them. We have established churches and Bible schools in 23 of those nations. All this has come about because I decided to do what Jesus did; He sacrificed His own desires in order to fulfill the Father's will.

If you will do the same thing, God will exalt you, no matter what circumstances you may face.

Think of it in terms of sowing and reaping. *"Whatsoever a man soweth, that shall he also reap. And let us not be weary in well doing: for in due season we shall reap, if we faint not"* (Gal. 6:7,9).

Habakkuk 2:3 will further encourage you: *"For the vision is yet for an appointed time, but at the end it shall speak, and not lie: though it tarry, wait for it; because it will **surely** come."*

Be encouraged that your faithfulness has not gone unnoticed. The Father sees the things you do in the background to fulfill the vision of your leader—things that not even your leader knows about—and He promises to reward you openly (Matt. 6:4). Hang in there. In due season you will reap if you faint not!

Developing the Spirit of an Armorbearer

- Meditate on the verses mentioned in the devotion and allow them to encourage you.

- Refuse to give place to discouragement, self-pity, envy, or jealousy.

- Proclaim it out loud!

- Plant a "seed" of action, finances, or prayer into your leader's vision today.

- Rejoice in the Lord!

Heavenly Father, You know the dreams and desires of my heart, dreams that You have given me. I work so hard to help my leader fulfill the vision You've given him, and I do it joyfully. Sometimes, though, it seems that my own desires have been put on hold or that they no longer even matter. But I rely on Your promises. Thank You that if I don't become weary or faint in well doing, in due season the dreams You have given me will be fulfilled and I will reap a harvest of blessing. Amen.

WALKING IN LOVE

Do whatever they tell you—not only if they are kind and reasonable, but even if they are harsh. For God is pleased with you when, for the sake of your conscience, you patiently endure unfair treatment....If you suffer for doing right and are patient beneath the blows, God is pleased with you. ...Christ, who suffered for you, is your example. Follow in his steps. He never sinned.... He did not retaliate when he was insulted. When he suffered, he did not threaten to get even. He left his case in the hands of God, who always judges fairly (see 1 Peter 2:18-23 NLT)

An armorbearer must possess endless strength so as to thrust, press, and force his way onward without giving way under harsh treatment.

The passage above makes it very clear that there will be times in the midst of battle when you and I will feel that we are being wrongfully treated. These types of situations are bound to arise, but do not allow satan to put resentment into your heart. Learn to give the situation over to the Lord and endure what comes patiently; God will be pleased with you.

It may be that in your heart you know you made the right decision, but in the eyes of your leader, it may seem wrong. Such times will develop character in you if you will walk in love and allow the Spirit of God to take charge of the matter. Your strength will always come by encouraging yourself in the Lord, as David did in First Samuel 30:6.

The easy thing to do is to quit, saying, "Well, no one around here appreciates me; I was rebuked, and I know I was right in what I did." Do not give in to the flesh. Avoid the temptation to sow discord by telling others of your plight. God sees all, and you must trust Him to make things right.

The best thing you can do is to go into your prayer closet and stay there until First Peter 2:20 has become a part of your very being. In time, victory will spring forth and your heart will rejoice once again.

Developing the Spirit of an Armorbearer

- Are you in the midst of a situation like what is described here? If so, separate yourself for a season of prayer. Pour your heart out to God. It might help to write down your thoughts and feelings.

- Give God the care of the situation and receive His boundless love and healing. Then out of that overflow, forgive your leader.

- Walk in love at all times.

Dear God, I make mistakes like everyone, but this time I know that I did what was right, what You wanted me to do. I refuse to give in to anger and self-pity, and I commit the situation to You, for You are my defense. I pray for my leader and trust that You are at work in Him. Make things right between us and bless him. Amen.

FOLLOWING THE LEADER

For I [a centurion] also am a man set under authority, having under me soldiers, and I say unto one, Go, and he goeth; and to another, Come, and he cometh; and to my servant, Do this, and he doeth it (Luke 7:8).

An armorbearer must follow orders immediately and correctly. In order for a person to ever become a good leader, he must first be a good follower; and being a good follower means taking care of things quickly and efficiently. If you aspire to become a leader, then the one you serve today must be able to depend upon you to carry out his directives. I'd like to share some simple keys to help you become a better follower so that someday you may become a good leader.

First, write everything down. I know what you're probably thinking: *Boy, what a revelation!* But let's be practical. God had everything written down for us, so we would not forget anything. We dare not do any less for ourselves. Write down the orders of your leader just as a waiter writes down an order for food. Make sure your leader gets *exactly what he orders*.

Second, ask him to explain anything you don't understand.

Third, make sure you have the correct information before you leave to carry out the order. It is a good idea to repeat the directive back to your leader. For example, you could say, "You are asking me to do thus and so by such and such a time." Many times we misrepresent our leader because we misunderstand what he means.

Finally, treat your leader's orders as highest priority. When asked to do something, do it immediately! I am always blessed when my secretary is efficient. Her efficiency ministers to me. The same results will come when you put your heart into carrying out instructions quickly and correctly.

Developing the Spirit of an Armorbearer

If you are not in the habit of doing the things mentioned above, make yourself a small checklist of the four points and carry it with you. Perhaps you could post it in your day planner so that it is readily visible. Refer to it when receiving any directives from your leader. After you've done this for a while, it will become second nature and you will be an incredibly efficient asset to your leader.

Father God, I am determined to be the best follower that I can be. Help me to keep these suggestions in mind and put them into practice often. Help me to get it right the first time, just the way my leader intends. Amen.

SUPPORTING THE LEADER

Greet Priscilla and Aquila my helpers in Christ Jesus: who have for my life laid down their own necks (Romans 16:3-4).

Every leader needs a group of faithful supporters, especially among his associates and staff, and his armorbearer should be the chief one. The word *support* means "to hold up or serve as a foundation for; uphold; advocate; champion."[1]

Contrary to popular belief, leaders are human just like anyone else. They hurt; they make mistakes; they get frustrated and bothered; many times they face discouragement and disappointment. Your job as an armorbearer is to uphold, sustain, maintain, and defend your leader, to be there for him to lean on in times of need.

Right now, as I am writing this, I am laughing because I can just hear the voice of some staff member or associate crying out: "What about *me*? What about *my* hurts, wounds, and problems?" Sure, an armorbearer has his share of hurts and disappointments, but to fulfill his duty to his leader, he must set aside his own problems and lay his life down for the leader. The armorbearer must cast his cares on the Lord and trust Him to take care of his hurts and frustrations.

Then there are those associates whose only desire and goal is to stand up in front of people and preach. They want to be in front of the leader—until war breaks out; then they suddenly jump behind him! God has called you and me to go out in front of our leader for only one reason, and that is to raise up our shield of faith and protect him from the harmful words of people and the fiery darts of the devil.

You will never make any real progress toward leadership until you have first mastered the art of supporting your spiritual leader. But you can master it and be an invaluable source of strength to him.

Developing the Spirit of an Armorbearer

- What issues are you dealing with in your personal life?

- Are you tempted to seek support from your leader regarding them?

- If you haven't already done so, find three or four Scriptures that pertain to your situation. Meditate on these verses and talk to God about them, thanking

Him for the answers they provide. Pour your heart out to your Father, because He cares about you far more than your leader or any earthly person can—and He is the miracle worker!

• If the issues are interfering with your ability to serve your leader, seek support from a Christian counselor or other godly leader.

Heavenly Father, thank You for being there in my hour of need. Thank You that I can come boldly to Your throne and pour out my heart to You at any time. Thank You for the promises You have given me in Your Word and that You watch over them to perform them for me. You are perfecting those things that concern me, and I take comfort in that. If my problems become too overwhelming and interfere with my ability to serve my leader in the way he needs, lead me to a godly believer who can advise me wisely, will pray for me according to Your Word, and can be trusted to keep my situation confidential. Amen.

Endnote

1. *The Merriam-Webster Dictionary*, 1998, s.v. "support."

BEING AN EXCELLENT COMMUNICATOR

Let your speech be always with grace, seasoned with salt, that ye may know how ye ought to answer every man (Colossians 4:6).

Communication is more important than anything I know of in establishing a relationship between an armorbearer and his leader. It is the only way to build trust between the leader and his associates. This does not mean that you are to bother your leader with every issue or decision that comes up, just that you should let him be aware of what is going on in the church or ministry and among the people.

In my years of service as an associate minister, I learned a very valuable lesson: *never hide anything from your leader.* Always let him know if someone is having (or causing) a problem in the church or ministry and what steps you are taking to resolve that situation.

Many times I have had to deal with things that I know are clearly in my area of responsibility, but I always make my leader aware of what I am doing. Situations will sometimes arise that I know should be dealt with by the leader himself. When that happens, I let him know about them. Either he will deal with the situations, or he will give me advice as to how to handle them.

The bottom line is communication.

If anyone ever says to you, "I want to tell you something in private, but you must promise not to let the leader know I told you about it," you should stop that conversation immediately and say to the person, "I am sorry, but I cannot make any such promise."

You owe it to your leader to reveal anything that is going to cause problems in the church. Jesus said that there is nothing hidden that will not be revealed (Mark 4:22). If you withhold something from your leader, then I can safely prophesy that it will come back on you. It will blow up, and you will be caught in the middle of the explosion. Secrecy is a trap that satan lays for the unsuspecting. Don't fall into it.

Developing the Spirit of an Armorbearer

Meditate and act on the following verses:

- *"Hear; for I will speak of excellent things; and the opening of my lips shall be right things. For my mouth shall*

speak truth; and wickedness is an abomination to my lips. All the words of my mouth are in righteousness; there is nothing forward or perverse in them" (Proverbs 8:6-8).

- *"Righteous lips are the delight of kings; and they love him that speaketh right"* (Proverbs 16:13).

- *"The lips of the righteous know what is acceptable: but the mouth of the wicked speaketh forwardness"* (Proverbs 10:31-32).

- *"For lack of wood the fire goes out, and where there is no whisperer, contention quiets down"* (Proverbs 26:20 NASB).

- *"Reliable communication permits progress"* (Proverbs 13:17 TLB).

Dear God, I want to be an excellent communicator and am committed to being one. I ask You to give me wisdom about the things I need to communicate to my leader and what things do not require his attention. I will not hide anything from my leader or take part in any conversation where I am asked to do so. Help me and my leader to keep the lines of communication open between us, and help us avoid any misunderstanding. Help me to keep my communication positive and to the point. Jesus is Lord over our communication. Amen.

GAINING VICTORIES
FOR THE LEADER

A wicked messenger falls into trouble, but a trustworthy envoy brings healing (Proverbs 13:17 NIV).

The armorbearer must have a disposition that will eagerly gain victories for his leader.

In Second Samuel 22:36, David said of the Lord, *"Thy gentleness hath made me great."* David was a great warrior. But instead of declaring that it was his boldness, assurance, or strength that made him great, he said that it was God's gentleness. This characteristic will gain victories for the leader and the one who serves him as armorbearer. Armed with this attitude, you will represent your leader well and gain much favor for both of you.

Always remember that as an armorbearer, wherever you go and whatever you do, you represent your leader. You do not want to do anything to bring a reproach to him or the ministry you both serve.

I have seen times when the leader has asked an associate to make unpopular changes in his department. Then that associate calls his staff together and tells them: "The leader has said that you had better straighten up or out you go." That makes a leader look as if he is some kind of unholy, ruthless king sitting on his throne, barking out orders.

This kind of thing happens often in ministries, and the result is always strife. The only reason any associate would say such a thing is to make it look as if he really cares for the people under him, but the leader doesn't. It is just an attempt to save his own reputation at the expense of the leader's. A true armorbearer will always strive to represent his leader well before all men.

When we work with people, we face many delicate situations every day. Even though you are not the shepherd of the flock or the head of the ministry, as an armorbearer you must take into your spirit the heart of a shepherd. You must learn to deal with people in love and find some common ground of agreement with the ones you work and deal with. No one is unreachable as long as he is teachable.

In my 23 years of experience as an associate, I have sat with people and explained to them what my leader meant by a statement he had made. Some people are easily offended, and many times they will come to the associate before going directly to the leader. I tried to help them understand what the leader really meant because I knew his heart. From there, if they were still upset, I encouraged them to make an appointment to meet with him personally to discuss the matter.

I encourage you to trust God every day for a spirit of humility, meekness, forgiveness, and purity and a clear conscience. These virtues will keep a guard around you and enable you to represent your leader well, causing you to be a real asset to the ministry.

Developing the Spirit of an Armorbearer

- Consider how you represent your leader to others, especially when it comes to discussing something that is unpopular. Do you convey your leader in a negative light and distance yourself from his decisions? Or do you make the effort to relay his words in a loving and uplifting manner, taking the time to explain the leader's heart in the matter?

- Make the commitment to be a peacemaker and a faithful ambassador.

Based on James 3:17 (NIV), I receive the wisdom that comes from Heaven. Because I allow it to flow through me, I am pure and love peace. I am considerate toward those under my direction and submissive to my leader. I am full of mercy and good fruit. I am impartial and sincere and a peacemaker who sows in peace. As a

result, I raise a harvest of righteousness in the ministry I serve. Amen.

MINISTERING TO
THE LEADER

[Stephanas, Fortunatus, and Achaicus] have cheered me [Paul] and have been a wonderful encouragement to me, as I am sure they were to you, too (1 Corinthians 16:18 TLB).

An armorbearer must have the ability to minister strength and courage to his leader. In order to do this, an armorbearer must possess an endless fountain of these virtues himself. The word *courage* means "the ability to conquer fear or despair; bravery; valor."[1]

When your leader stands up and says, "Thus saith the Lord, 'Build the church building without going into debt,'" what is your reaction?

Some may say, "The leader is really missing it this time."

How do you respond?

Remember when the children of Israel were told to go into the Promised Land and overcome it (Num. 13). They sent 12 spies into the land who came back and reported on what they had seen there. Only two had the courage to say, *"Let's go up and take it, for we are well able to do so"* (Num. 13:30). Everyone else said, "No, we can't do it."

Whenever God speaks to your Moses, be like Joshua and Caleb, the two strong, courageous spies. Stand up in faith and courage and go forth to take the land—no matter how big the task may be.

Courage comes from faith in God. In order to walk in the same assurance your leader has and to be an encouragement and strength to him, you must stay built up in the Word of God. This edification comes only by putting the Word first. When you do, you will be a dynamic force for the leader you serve.

Developing the Spirit of an Armorbearer

- Read Numbers 13 and consider the attitudes of the fearful spies as well as the courage of Joshua and Caleb. With whom do you most identify? Repent of any doubt, fear, and unbelief, and begin to proclaim courage based on God's promises regarding the situation.

- Develop a "can-do" spirit. Meditate and act on the following: *"Be strong and of a good courage, fear not, nor be afraid of them: for the Lord thy God, he it is that doth go with thee; he will not fail thee, nor forsake thee"* (Deut. 31:6).

> *"This book of the law shall not depart out of thy mouth; but thou shalt meditate therein day and night, that thou mayest observe to do according to all that is written therein: for then thou shalt make thy way prosperous, and then thou shalt have good success. Have not I commanded thee? Be strong and of a good courage; be not afraid, neither be thou dismayed: for the Lord thy God is with thee whithersoever thou goest"* (Joshua 1:8-9).

> *"Wait on the Lord: be of good courage, and he shall strengthen thine heart: wait, I say, on the Lord"* (Psalm 27:14).

> *"I can do all things through Christ which strengtheneth me"* (Philippians 4:13).

Heavenly Father, I praise You for the plans and purposes You have called my leader to accomplish, and I thank You for the privilege of being called alongside to help him. I will be strong in You and the power of Your might so that I may be a strength and encouragement to him. I will only speak words of faith and confidence, for I put my trust in You. By Your Word, we will go forth and possess the land. Amen.

Endnote

1. *The Merriam-Webster Dictionary*, 1998, s.v. "courage."

TEMPTATIONS
TO OVERCOME

BELIEVING YOU ARE
THE LEADER'S REPLACEMENT

Like the coolness of snow at harvest time is a trustworthy messenger to those who send him; he refreshes the spirit of his masters (Proverbs 25:13 NIV).

My pastor understood the calling and anointing on my life when I served as his armorbearer, and it was his desire to see that calling fulfilled. Moreover, I understood my God-given duties to stand with him and help him fulfill the vision God had given both of us. I understood that I had to fully submit myself to him.

For the leader/armorbearer relationship to work as God intends, this type of trust must be developed. On the one hand, the armorbearer must be confident that it is God's will that he serve under this particular leader, and he must also trust the leader himself. On the other hand, the leader must trust that his armorbearer is looking out for his (the leader's) best interest. The leader must be able to trust that his armorbearer is not seeking to replace him or steal the sheep entrusted to the leader's care.

This type of trust takes time to develop. Sadly, too often today the trust between leader and armorbearer has been violated. As a result, there can be no flow between them.

It is vital that the armorbearer guard against the temptation to believe he is called to replace the leader. In Numbers 13 and 14, we read about a biblical example of this. When the faithless, fearful children of Israel heard the bad report of the ten spies who had been sent to spy out the land of Canaan, they cried out, *"Let us make a captain, and let us return into Egypt"* (Num. 14:4). As a result, they exasperated Moses, Aaron, and the faith-filled spies, Joshua and Caleb.

In ministries today, many times the first choice of a new captain will be the associate minister. When a portion of the people begin to call out for you to become their new leader—beware. When they are ready to make you captain in place of the leader because you will lead them the way they want to go—look out! That is a deception and temptation from satan. It is not the way to success and life. It is the way into sin and rebellion, and God is never in such a movement.

Renew your commitment today to be a faithful and trustworthy armorbearer. Let your words and actions increase your leader's level of trust and confidence. Then the flow between you will increase and the ministry will flourish.

Developing the Spirit of an Armorbearer

- Have you faced the temptation to believe you are your leader's replacement? If so, do you see the trap of the enemy?

- Today, purposely say or do something that will reassure your leader of your commitment to support him.

- Meditate on these verses about trustworthiness: *"'Well done!' the king exclaimed. 'You are a trustworthy servant'"* (Luke 19:17 NLT).

  "I [Paul] am sending Timothy—to help you do this. For he is my beloved and trustworthy child in the Lord" (1 Corinthians 4:17 NLT).

  "How thankful I am to Christ Jesus our Lord for considering me trustworthy and appointing me to serve him" (1 Timothy 1:12 NLT).

  "Urge slaves to obey their masters and to try their best to satisfy them. They must not talk back, nor steal, but must show themselves to be entirely trustworthy. In this way they will make people want to believe in our Savior and God" (Titus 2:9-10 TLB).

Heavenly Father, I am committed to being a trustworthy armorbearer to my leader. I refuse to give place to thoughts of replacing my leader or on starting my own ministry and taking sheep with me. If You do ever call me to a new assignment, I trust You to reveal it to both my leader and me. Should that be Your plan, thank You

that it will be peaceable and a blessing to all concerned. Whether You've called me to this man for a lifetime or only a season, I will conduct myself as though this is my lifelong mission. Amen.

QUESTIONING THE
LEADER'S MOTIVES

*If you love someone, you will be loyal to him no matter
what the cost. You will always believe in him, always
expect the best of him, and always stand your ground in
defending him* (1 Corinthians 13:7 TLB).

Let's face it: satan is out to destroy the leader/armorbearer
relationship because he knows how powerful it is. A
common deception and temptation from satan that must be
guarded against and overcome is the false idea that the
leader is more concerned with fulfilling his own personal
vision than he is with meeting the needs of his associates and
staff members. The lie is that the leader will go to any lim-
its to accomplish his own goal, but will not go out of his way
to help meet the goals of those who work with him.

Remember one thing: The vision of the ministry you are
called to serve is God's vision, and if He did not think you
could fit in with it, He would never have placed you in that
ministry to begin with. You will not always get a pat on the

back for doing a good job. For believers, our rewards are waiting for us in Heaven. Would you prefer for your leader to pat you on the back and say, "Good job," or for Jesus to pat you on the back and say, *"Well done, good and faithful servant"* (Matt. 25:21)?

God is a wonderful accountant, and someday the books will be opened and the rewards distributed. I trust that your rewards will be great. They will be determined by your attitude here and now on this earth.

Developing the Spirit of an Armorbearer

Study and meditate on the following verses about rewards:

- *"And whatsoever ye do, do it heartily, as to the Lord, and not unto men; Knowing that of the Lord ye shall receive the reward of the inheritance: for ye serve the Lord Christ"* (Colossians 3:23-24).

- *"For the Son of man shall come in the glory of his Father with his angels; and then he shall reward every man according to his works"* (Matthew 16:27).

- *"For whosoever shall give you a cup of water to drink in my name, because ye belong to Christ, verily I say unto you, he shall not lose his reward"* (Mark 9:41).

- *"Now he that planteth and he that watereth are one: and every man shall receive his own reward according to his*

own labor. For we are laborers together with God"
(1 Corinthians 3:8-9).

Dear God, I am here to serve my leader. Forgive me for those times that I've desired or even sought for his approval. Of course, I want to do those things that bless him, but I realize my reward comes from You. First and foremost I want to please You. When I do that, my leader can't help but be blessed. I am committed to conduct myself in such a way that when I meet You face to face, You will say, "Well done, thou good and faithful servant." Amen.

OLD-TESTAMENT
ARMORBEARERS

ABIMELECH'S ARMORBEARER

Never let loyalty and kindness get away from you! Wear them like a necklace; write them deep within your heart. Then you will find favor with both God and people, and you will gain a good reputation (Proverbs 3:3- 4 NLT).

A good example of the loyalty of an armorbearer is found in the story of the death of Abimelech (Judg. 9:45-55).

This event took place during a war in which Abimelech was laying siege to a city. He was succeeding in his attempt to seize the city and had the enemy on the run. When he came to a tower where many of the people had taken refuge, he was prepared to burn it down. As wood was being laid at the foot of the tower, a woman in the top threw down a piece of millstone that struck Abimelech on the head, cracking his skull. He went to his armorbearer and ordered the young man, *"Draw thy sword, and slay me, that men say not of me, A woman slew him"* (Judg. 9:54).

Even though Abimelech was wicked, the loyalty of his armorbearer is obvious. He was the closest person to the king when the stone struck him on the head. He was just as concerned about Abimelech's tainted honor as Abimelech was himself. He did not want it said that his officer had been killed by a woman. His instant obedience is also recorded: *"And his young man thrust him through, and he died"* (Judg. 9:54).

Most likely you and your leader will not encounter such a dramatic turn of events; however, this armorbearer set a wonderful example from which you can glean. Notice:

- This armorbearer was loyal and dedicated to an undeserving, evil king. He stayed true to his calling regardless of any other factor.

- This armorbearer was as concerned about his leader's honor as his leader was.

- He was instantly obedient.

Developing the Spirit of an Armorbearer

As you consider the three important attributes of this armorbearer, evaluate your relationship with your leader in the same areas.

- Upon what is your loyalty to your leader based? Simply your assignment from God? How do your leader's actions, character, and belief system affect your loyalty? What other factors are involved?

- Is the honor of your leader one of your chief concerns? Does this concern carry over into your actions? How?

- Are you instantly obedient, or do you question directives given to you? Do you argue or complain internally or to others?

Father God, if this Old Testament armorbearer could be so loyal to an evil king, surely I can be equally as loyal and obedient to the leader You've commissioned me to support. When times get tough, help me to recognize ways to honor him and show my loyalty to him. Amen.

Note: If a leader falls into sin or heresy, an armorbearer should look to God and other strong leaders to help in the restoration process. Rejoice at the repentance and the restoring of your leader to his God-called office. If the leader turns from any method of restoration, then a decision must be made as to whether you should break the relationship. An armorbearer's loyalty is to God and the Word first. In this situation, you must look to the Lord for direction and keep yourself from any slanderous spirit. Continue in prayer for God to bring change to your leader's heart.

Ways To Preserve Your Leader's Honor

- Pray—stay in prayer for his restoration.

- Love—let him know that you love him but cannot condone the sin.

- Understanding—gain understanding from the situation.

- Examine your own heart, and make a clear decision not to fall into the sin yourself.

- Don't compromise—under no circumstance should you compromise your standards or values that are based on the Word of God.

- Stay in faith—keep in mind that your leader can turn back to God at any time and God will heal him. Be ready with open arms to help if he turns to you.

SAUL'S ARMORBEARER

See my servant….He will not break the bruised reed, nor quench the dimly burning flame. He will encourage the fainthearted, those tempted to despair (Isaiah 42:1-2 TLB).

In First Samuel 31:4-6 and First Chronicles 10:4-5, we read that Saul and his army were fighting against the Philistines and losing ground. Saul's army, realizing that defeat was imminent, turned to flee. His men—including his sons—were killed, and Saul was wounded by arrows. He turned to his armorbearer and ordered him: *"Draw thy sword, and thrust me though therewith; lest these uncircumcised come and thrust me through, and abuse me"* (1 Sam. 31:4).

Saul wanted to die at the hands of his armorbearer rather than be captured and tortured by the enemy. However, his armorbearer would not oblige him, so Saul took his own life by falling on his sword. *"And when his armorbearer saw that Saul was dead, he fell likewise upon his sword, and died with him"* (1 Sam. 31:5).

When Saul commanded his faithful servant to thrust him through with his sword, *"his armorbearer would not; for he was sore afraid"* (1 Sam. 31:4). It seems peculiar that an armorbearer would be "sore afraid." He had been selected, trained, and prepared to serve in battle. Because he was an armorbearer to the king, he was probably more skilled in warfare than any other soldier in the king's army. His duty was to protect the commander-in-chief. It doesn't seem logical that a man who was trained and prepared to give his life to save and defend the king would be afraid.

In the Hebrew, this word translated "afraid" in the King James Version is *yare' (yaw-ray')*. It does not mean to be afraid in the sense of being frightened or terrorized, but to fear out of *reverence!* In this case, it means *"to sorely respect and honor"!*

Now the armorbearer's reaction is much more understandable.

This man had spent all his time in Saul's service, caring for and protecting him. His entire reason for being was the preservation of the life of the king. If there was even the slightest chance that Saul could be saved from destruction, then he had to take that chance, regardless of the odds against its success.

Perhaps it was just too much to ask of the man who had protected Saul all this time to take the very life he had pledged to defend. He just could not bring himself to destroy the one he had spent his life preserving and protecting.

When your leader feels like throwing in the towel, do you "sorely respect and honor" him to the point that you would do everything in your power to stop him? You can see how important it is for you stay built up on the Word of God in order to keep hope alive and your faith unshakable. Your confident expectation for good may be the very thing your leader needs to get him through a tough spot when all hope seems lost.

Developing the Spirit of an Armorbearer

- Make sure you have the leader's God-given vision in writing and that it is posted in a highly visible place for all—especially your leader—to see (Hab. 2:2). Keep it in the forefront of your thoughts.

- Absolutely *refuse* to speak any words of doubt or unbelief regarding the situation. *"Be steadfast, unmovable, always abounding in the work of the Lord"* (1 Cor. 15:58).

- Voice your confidence in your leader and the assurance that God always causes him to triumph in Christ (2 Cor. 2:14).

Heavenly Father, it would be so easy for me to become discouraged and give up like my leader wants to, but I

cannot afford that luxury. My leader is depending on me to remain "steadfast, unmovable." I refuse to give any place to the devil by uttering any words of doubt or unbelief. Against hope I believe in hope and will remain faithful to my leader until we see the victory, for it shall surely come, in Jesus' name. Amen.

JONATHAN'S ARMORBEARER

And [Jonathan's] armorbearer said unto him, Do all that is in thine heart: turn thee; behold, I am with thee according to thy heart (1 Samuel 14:7).

In First Samuel 14:1–23 there is another account of a relationship between a young man and his armorbearer. Jonathan ordered his armorbearer to accompany him over to the garrison of the Philistines against whom he and the other Israelites were warring. He wanted to go over single-handed. Jonathan had not told his father, Saul, of his intentions. Though the king knew nothing about the plan, and though he and his master were only two against an entire army, Jonathan's armorbearer obeyed.

In verse 6, Jonathan says, *"Come, and let us go over unto the garrison of these uncircumcised: it may be that the Lord will work for us: for there is no restraint to the Lord to save by many or by few."* It was then that the young and fearless armorbearer spoke the words in our text: *"Do all that is in thine heart: turn thee; behold, I am with thee according to thy heart."*

As the two young men climbed up toward the enemy's camp, God confirmed to them that He had, in fact, delivered the enemy into their hand. Jonathan turned to his companion and said, *"Come up after me"* (1 Sam. 14:12).

When they reached the place where the enemy was standing, *"they fell before Jonathan; and his armorbearer slew after him"* (1 Sam. 14:13). God saved the whole nation of Israel that day through the brave actions of Jonathan and his faithful, obedient armorbearer.

It is curious to note that in verse 6 Jonathan said, *"It may be that the Lord will work for us."* Although Jonathan was not certain about what would happen, his armorbearer was more than willing to follow. Verse 7, our text verse, reveals his answer and the proper attitude of any armorbearer: *"Do all that is in thine heart: turn thee; behold, I am with thee according to thy heart."*

As they approached the enemy, Jonathan's armorbearer knew his place—to come *after* Jonathan. In verse 13, we see that it was the anointing upon Jonathan—the anointing of a leader—that caused the enemy to fall. The young armorbearer was diligent to follow along *after* his officer, destroying the enemy who had been knocked to the ground by God's anointing upon his leader: *"and his armorbearer slew after him"* (1 Sam. 14:13).

This is a classic example of the humility and diligence of a biblical armorbearer. He is one who wins victories and slays enemies while his leader gets the glory. He is the one who trusts his officer, one who takes his place *behind* the man he serves, not striving to get out in front.

Developing the Spirit of an Armorbearer

- Does your heart mirror the disposition and sentiment of the heart of Jonathan's armorbearer?

  "Do all that is in your mind; I am with you in whatever you think [best]" (AMP)

  "Do all that you have in mind...Go ahead; I am with you heart and soul" (NIV).

  "Whatever you want to do, I am with you" (GNB). *"Fine!...Do as you think best; I'm with you heart and soul, whatever you decide"* (TLB).

- Do you know your place, as Jonathan's armorbearer did? Are you willing to serve *behind* your leader, to allow him to be the one out front, the one who gets the credit?

Father God, I consider it a privilege to serve behind my leader because it is the place You've call me to be. Like Jonathan's armorbearer, I want to be fully supportive of my leader, to encourage him to do all that is in his heart. I pray that his heart would be filled only with what You put there and not merely human ideas. Thank You that he knows Your voice and the voice of a stranger he will not follow. Thank You also for working in him to will and to do of Your good pleasure. Amen.

DAVID AS ARMORBEARER

Behold, I have seen a son of Jesse the Bethlehemite, that is cunning in playing; and a mighty valiant man, and a man of war, and prudent in matters, and a comely person, and the Lord is with him (1 Samuel 16:18).

In First Samuel 16:14-23 we find the story of the last of the four armorbearers.

King Saul was troubled. He had a distressing spirit and decided to find a skillful musician who could ease his oppressed state of mind. David was the young man recommended to the king by one of his servants.

David was sent to Saul, bearing gifts, and we are told that Saul *"loved him greatly"* and made him his armorbearer (1 Sam. 16:21.) He could minister strength to Saul, causing him to feel "refreshed" and "well" (1 Sam. 16:23). In verse 18, the young armorbearer was described as follows:

• Skillful in playing

- A mighty man of valor
- A man of war
- Prudent in speech
- Handsome in appearance
- One whom the Lord was with

All of these qualities are biblical descriptions of a true armorbearer. Perhaps the fact that David had once been Saul's armorbearer further explains his attitude when he later declared that he would not touch *"the Lord's anointed"* (1 Sam. 26:9). No matter how hard Saul tried to kill David or how many opportunities David had to slay Saul, David never struck back.

Did David walk in the same reverential fear that caused Saul's future armorbearer to refuse to kill him? More than likely, yes. This respect and honor toward God's anointed may also explain David's attitude of extreme repentance, sorrow, and humility before Saul after he had sneaked up behind the king in a cave and cut off the edge of his robe (1 Sam. 24:1-6).

David was a true armorbearer, one who held no grudges but faithfully and obediently withstood his captain's harsh treatment. The result was his eventual promotion to his own place of high respect and honor.

Developing the Spirit of an Armorbearer

Review the description of David above and evaluate how your leader and others would describe you. Make any necessary adjustments.

- Are you skillful at your craft?

- Are you a mighty man of valor?

- Are you proficient in spiritual warfare?

- Are you prudent in speech and pleasant in appearance?

- Do you "touch not" God's anointed?

- Do you readily repent and operate in humility?

- Do you walk in love and refuse to hold grudges when treated harshly?

- Is it obvious to others that the Lord is with you?

Heavenly Father, I want to be an armorbearer of excellence. You know what is in my heart, but I want these characteristics to abound in me so that they are apparent to all. I am committed to having the same respect and humility toward my leader that David had toward Saul, regardless of anything my leader says or does. And I pray for my leader, that these characteristics would abound in him as well so that he will never get off track and go the way of Saul. I trust You to keep him. Amen.

ARMORBEARING IN
THE NEW TESTAMENT

SETTING PRIORITIES

Thou shalt love the Lord thy God with all thy heart, and with all thy soul, and with all thy mind. This is the first and great commandment (Matthew 22:37-38).

Thus far we have investigated the Old Testament concerning the subject of armorbearing, and we have clearly defined the duty, role, and service of the armorbearer in his Old Testament function. Now let's look more closely at this role of armorbearing in the light of the New Testament.

In the life of every Christian, God has established a certain order of priorities. Both the armorbearer and the person he is serving should follow these priorities if they are to live fruitful Christian lives. In descending order of importance, these priorities are:

1. Relationship with God

2. Relationship with spouse

3. Relationship with children

4. Employment or work

One of the main differences between armorbearing in the Old Testament and in the New Testament is the fact that in Old Testament days, the duty of an armorbearer was priority number one. In the New Testament, armorbearing is priority number four.

Keeping one's relationship with God fresh and thriving is the basis for all of the other areas of life flowing smoothly. How easy it is, though, to let the duties of the ministry or work come before all of the other areas. It is something every believer must guard against. It brings no honor to God when the family unit breaks down because of a neglected marriage. And how could it possibly bring glory to God when a person's children rebel against the things of God because the needs of the ministry have pushed them out of the way?

This doesn't mean that today's armorbearer is to take less than necessary care of his responsibility, however. His position is a God-given one, and he must be a good steward of that duty. The physical roles may have changed, but the attitude of the heart must be the same.

It is not easy to keep priorities straight and to walk in excellence in each area, but it is vital if the armorbearer is to reach his full potential. Adjustments may need to be made from time to time, but the fruit that results from it will be fruit that remains and brings glory to God.

Developing the Spirit of an Armorbearer

- You may agree on the order in which each priority should fall, but what is the reality in your life? You may want God to be number one, but is He? Are you giving your spouse and children the priority treatment they need?

- What safeguards can you put into place to ensure that you keep your priorities in line?

- If you have been putting your role as armorbearer ahead of other areas, what are some things you can do to ensure that even though you are moving it to position number four, you can still perform your armor-bearing duties with excellence?

Father, life sure can be a juggling act. I find it difficult to keep my priorities in line when life is so fast paced. The urgent things try to monopolize my time and push the important things to the side. I want to excel in each of the four areas of my life and live in such a way that everything I do brings glory to You. I must have Your wisdom in order to do that, and I receive it now. Help me to walk in the Spirit moment by moment and to allow You to show me the path of life. Amen.

DIVINE APPOINTMENT,
NOT A STEPPING STONE

Let us run with patience the race that is set before us
(Hebrews 12:1).

An issue that needs to be addressed is the mind-set that armorbearing is merely a stepping stone to a position in leadership. We have seen this happen so many times in the Body of Christ, and it is a reproach to God. If a person feels that the only reason God has him where he is now is so he can be promoted to "something bigger and better," then, it's sad to say, that individual is operating in the world's system. The determining factor for this type of individual is the amount of money or authority that comes with the position. The highest bidder wins out.

Did you ever stop and ask God if your current position is the one He has chosen for you, if where you are now is where He wants you to be? It makes no difference what the salary or working conditions are; what really matters is whether God has called you to that job and place.

While serving my pastor, I had two opportunities to become the pastor of another church. Both of these were good churches, and at the time of the offers, the pay would have been better than what I was receiving where I was. Besides all that, I could have been the senior pastor, rather than an associate. If I had operated by the world's system, I would have jumped at the chance for "advancement." But the Kingdom of God does not operate that way.

I know that I am in God's *divinely appointed* position for me, and that is the key. When people come to join the staff in our ministry, I pray, "Lord, send us the people who are divinely appointed by You to be here to work with us."

Unless a leader's staff are divinely *called* and *sent* to him by the Lord, he doesn't want them. I understand that there will be times when God will separate a person from his current position. That moment may come for you one day. But if it does come, God's best is that both you and your leader will know in your spirit that it is time for a change. Then the separation will be best for all concerned. It will be best for the Kingdom of God.

Developing the Spirit of an Armorbearer

- Have you been divinely appointed to your position as armorbearer? How do you know? Take the time to write down your answers because they will be a great encouragement to you if you are offered other positions and when storms inevitably arise.

- Do you see your position as a stepping stone? If so, seek the Lord about it and make sure you view the position as He does.

- Whether or not you will be called to a different position someday, the important thing is that you give your current position your all today, as though you are called to serve there from now on. Do it joyfully!

Dear God, I realize the importance of serving in the role that You have divinely appointed for me. Unless You show me otherwise, I assume that I am in the position You've ordained for me for the rest of my life. Today I renew my commitment to serve my leader with my whole heart and to perform my duties in a manner that will bless him and honor You. If You ever want to move me to a different position or ministry, I trust You to make it clear to both me and my leader, and I trust You to help us make the transition smoothly. Amen.

BLOOM WHERE
YOU ARE PLANTED

Jesus said, "I have set you an example that you should do as I have done for you" (John 13:15 NIV).

On my office wall hangs a plaque that reads: "Bloom where you are planted." My life is a testimony that this biblical principle works. As armorbearers we must prove ourselves faithful where God has "planted" us. Let God exalt and promote you where you are. If you will be diligent, faithful, humble, and motivated by the heart of a servant, you will find the principles of God's Word working for you. As you humble yourself before God, He will exalt you (1 Pet. 5:6).

I would like to share an interesting story with you as an illustration of faithful armorbearing. Some years ago, my pastor met with the Billy Graham crusade team, which was planning a series of meetings in our city. The crusade coordinator began his talk by stating that he had been with Billy

Graham the least amount of time of any of the ministers on the staff—*23 years!*

When I heard about that, I was shocked. In charismatic circles, we preach faithfulness and staying with something, but the Billy Graham crusade team *lives* it. I got on my face before God and prayed, "Lord, if it is Your desire that I stay here as my pastor's armorbearer and serve this ministry in that capacity for the rest of my life, then Your will be done." One thing I knew was that if God ever said it was time for me to move on to another position, my pastor and I both would know it—and we did.

Some staff members and ministers are ready to give up and go on to their reward if God doesn't open up something new and better for them every year. We must start seeing our position as one called and instituted of God. We must be willing to stay in it for the rest of our lives, if that is what God wants.

If you are an associate or staff minister, I want to encourage you to remain faithful, no matter what pressure you may be facing. I honestly admit that there were times when I was serving as associate pastor that I wanted to throw in the towel and say, "This is too hard; this is not fair." But one day Jesus spoke to me and told me that He was simply asking me to do the same thing He had done on the earth. Jesus fulfilled His Father's desire and not His own. He is not asking you and me to do anything He Himself has not already done.

At this moment in my life, I am doing more than I have ever done for God, and I believe it is because I have bloomed wherever God has planted me. If you are being challenged in this area, but you know you are in the center of God's will, be determined to continue blooming where you are planted. Don't get ahead of God, and don't allow the devil or circumstances to pressure you out.

Stay right in the center of God's will and continue blooming where you are planted. You may not understand it now, but years from now when you look back in hindsight, you'll be glad you did.

Developing the Spirit of an Armorbearer

Think about how Jesus humbled Himself by coming to the earth and how, out of obedience to His Father, He stayed "planted." Drawing strength from His example, rejoice in your current position, and reaffirm your commitment. Jesus paid a huge price, but He also received a great reward. The reward for your obedience will be great too.

God, sometimes when I think I will be here forever, I want to bolt and run somewhere new and different. But I know You have me here for a reason. I will follow Jesus' example and choose Your will over my own. I am encouraged when I realize that my faithfulness will not

go unrewarded because You are a God of blessing. I will continue to bloom where I am planted. Amen.

DON'T GIVE UP!

And let us not be weary in well doing: for in due season we shall reap, if we faint not (Galatians 6:9).

One day a man came into my office, which is really nice. It has a beautiful view of a small mountain right behind my desk.

"Well," he said, "how does it feel to be a big man with a huge desk, leather chairs, and a view like you've got there?"

Thank the Lord I was in a good mood. People have no idea what it took to get to that place, although most staff ministers can relate to my feelings.

To answer the man's question, it feels today exactly as it felt in 1979, when my office had pea-green carpet, an army surplus desk, and a small window with a view of the back of a drug store. Did I complain? Heavens, no! My pastor had a door laid over two small filing cabinets for a desk. I was thrilled just to be able to say to someone, "Come into my office." It was ugly, but it was *my* office, the first real one I

105

had ever had. I had "birthed" it in the spirit in prayer, and I was as happy and proud of it as I could be.

The Spirit of God may be ministering to you right now because you are at the place of giving up in your ministry. Please don't! Get into the Word and start rejoicing in what you have been blessed with. Put your future into God's hands. Remember, David was faithful to Saul, and look how God exalted him.

One day it seemed like everything in the world was coming against me. I was discouraged. I felt left out. It seemed that God was just going to have to move me on. But I cried out to God for help and picked up my Bible, which fell open to Ephesians 5:17-19: *"Be ye not unwise, but understanding what the will of the Lord is....Be filled with the Spirit; speaking to yourselves in psalms and hymns and spiritual songs, singing and making melody in your heart to the Lord."*

As I read that passage, the Lord quickened the word "making" to me. *Son*, He said, *a piano makes beautiful music only when someone plays it. The joy, peace, and assurance you need are there, but you have to make the melody come forth. Get up and start dancing before Me.*

I did not feel like doing it, but I obeyed in faith and started leaping and jumping for joy, praising God. As I did so, the anointing broke the yoke of oppression.

If you are under a spirit of oppression, before you go any further, get up and start rejoicing. You are set free in Jesus' name. This is God's will for you right now.

Developing the Spirit of an Armorbearer

Whether you are discouraged or not, the following are good principles to follow to walk in victory:

- Have an attitude of gratitude for the good things God has blessed you with.

- Renew your commitment to be faithful where God has you.

- Encourage yourself with God's promises regarding the rewards for faithfulness, including the text verse.

- Follow David's example and rejoice in the Lord as an act of your will. Say Psalm 34:1-6 and Psalm 103:1-5 out loud so that you, God, and the devil can hear it.

Dear God, You know how things are for me right now. At times, it seems like the only answer is for me to leave, but even if that were Your will, I refuse to leave feeling like this. I refuse to quit. If You move me on, fine, but it will be after I gain the victory over this oppression. I put on the garment of praise for the spirit of heaviness. I will sing and dance and rejoice until the anointing begins to flow and this yoke of oppression is broken.

*Thank You, Father, for always causing me to triumph.
Amen.*

THE PERSONAL RELATIONSHIP
BETWEEN LEADER & ARMORBEARER

Now we ask you, brothers, to respect those who work hard among you, who are over you in the Lord and who admonish you. Hold them in the highest regard in love because of their work. Live in peace with each other (1 Thessalonians 5:12-13 NIV).

What about your personal relationship with your leader? In Second Corinthians 5:16, the apostle Paul says, *"Wherefore, henceforth know we no man after the flesh."* As an armorbearer, you have a called ministry to serve a general of God's army. The Old Testament suggests a very close physical relationship between the officer and his armorbearer. This may be the case in the New Testament too, but such a close personal relationship is not necessary to successfully carry out the responsibilities of the armorbearer. God did not call you to be your leader's fishing buddy. I was not called to be my pastor's best friend. We are friends, but that is not our primary relationship.

We should never assume a personal right to know or be a part of our leader's family or private life:

> Be not forward (self-assertive and boastfully ambitious) in the presence of the king, and stand not in the place of great men; For better it is that it be said to you, Come up here, than that you should be put lower in the presence of the prince whose eyes have seen you (Proverbs 25:6-7 AMP).

I will say this—a personal relationship of some kind is inevitable, but the armorbearer's primary role is not that of personal friend. The armorbearer's main purpose is to support his leader and to pull down satan's strongholds for him and the ministry. Do not get your feelings hurt if you are not asked to have dinner with the leader every Friday night. Your goal is not to get next to the leader but to get next to Jesus and to do battle in the Spirit for your leader.

Developing the Spirit of an Armorbearer

- How would you characterize your relationship with your leader? Is it warm emotionally or rather distant and cool? Either way, respecting your leader's boundaries is important if your leader is to trust you. Never be presumptuous of your leader or take liberties where your relationship is concerned.

- Show proper respect. The manner in which you relate to your leader should always reflect your position as a servant to him. This should hold true for as long as you are his armorbearer, even if your leader confides in you and at times relates to you as a friend.

Heavenly Father, thank You for the relationship my leader and I have. Out of respect for the office he holds, I will relate to him as my superior as long as I serve him. Help me to always show him proper respect and to recognize the boundaries that he has set so that I may honor them. Amen.

GODLY LEADERS NEED ASSISTANCE

As it is, there are many parts, but one body. The eye cannot say to the hand, "I don't need you!" And the head cannot say to the feet, "I don't need you!" On the contrary, those parts of the body that seem to be weaker are indispensable (1 Corinthians 12:20-22 NIV).

In the Old Testament, the armorbearer's main function was directly related to combat. This has not changed at all between the Old and New Testaments. What has changed greatly is the type of combat in which the New Testament armorbearer is to engage as he serves his officer.

"For we wrestle not against flesh and blood, but against principalities, against powers, against the rulers of the darkness of this world, against spiritual wickedness in high places" (Eph. 6:12). In this passage, we clearly see that we are not engaged in battle against the Philistines as the children of Israel were in the Old Testament. Under the New Covenant, we do not do battle against flesh and blood at all but against demonic powers.

God calls men and women to do great things and to accomplish wondrous tasks for Him. Preaching the Word of God to all nations is no small undertaking, and it is impossible for one person to accomplish it alone. That's where the Body of Christ comes in.

God places His vision inside a person and His anointing upon him to carry it forth. Then He surrounds that individual with other members of the Body of Christ to support and work with him toward the fulfillment of that vision. The Lord begins by sending armorbearers to assist the man of God and to take his spirit upon them. Their function is to do spiritual warfare for their leader and to take the load off him. They also help to impart his vision to the people. These individuals are the "indispensable" members of the Body of Christ that our text refers to. The leader cannot fulfill his mission without them.

Epaphroditus is a good New Testament example of what I am talking about. Paul acknowledges that Epaphroditus is his brother, his fellow worker, and his fellow soldier in the faith. He also acknowledges that the Philippian church had sent Epaphroditus to take care of his needs, or, we could say, to serve as his armorbearer (Phil. 2:25).

As strong in faith as the apostle Paul was, he still had need of those whom God sent to assist him. What a privilege it is to serve God's anointed. You are indispensable.

Developing the Spirit of an Armorbearer

- Be encouraged that you are an indispensable part of your leader's team. It is a divine calling to help take the load off him. What is something you can do today to lighten his load?

- Be able to verbalize your leader's vision to the people he is called to minister to as well as to any other armorbearers.

- Take seriously your assignment to pull down demonic strongholds. Continually take authority over them and forbid them to operate against your leader and his ministry. Surround your leader with a prayer covering of protection at all times.

Heavenly Father, what a wonderful vision You have given to the leader I serve, and I thank You for calling me alongside him to help fulfill it. I will be faithful to wage war in the spirit, to pull down the stronghold that would try to stop Your plan. I ask the Holy Spirit to help me remain vigilant and to recognize the first trace of demonic involvement. Not only will I pray, but I will also be faithful to assist my leader in any way he needs it. I serve at the pleasure of my King and for the good of my leader. Amen.

NO SECOND FIDDLE

*And those members of the body, which we think to be
less honorable, upon these we bestow more abundant
honor; and our uncomely parts have more abundant
comeliness* (1 Corinthians 12:23).

I have heard preachers refer to the associate ministry as
"playing second fiddle." I have a few questions that I
would like to ask those who think that way: Did Joshua play
second fiddle to Moses? Did Elisha play second fiddle to Elijah? Does a person's nose play second fiddle to his eyes?
Does his foot play second fiddle to his hand?

If you have thought of the associate ministry or other
support positions in this way, I hope that by now your
thinking has begun to change. *There is no second fiddle position in the Body of Christ.*

If anyone thinks that because he fills the position of pastor, prophet, apostle, evangelist, or teacher he is better than
the rest of the Body, then he had better prepare to be brought
low. That would be pride and will result in destruction,

according to Proverbs 16:18. I trust that you will never fall for that kind of deceptive thinking. As we've stated many times, God-called armorbearers are there to support the leader and to help fulfill the vision God has given him.

Many years ago, I told my pastor that I was behind him.

He stopped and said, "No, you are standing *with* me."

Our relationship did not reach that point overnight, but then, no meaningful relationship is built quickly. Your position in the ministry is important to God, and if you are faithful and patient, you will be exalted in due season.

Deuteronomy 32:30 says that one shall put a thousand to flight and two will chase ten thousand. With you by his side, your officer is ten times more powerful than he is alone. In Christ, there are no second fiddles.

Developing the Spirit of an Armorbearer

- Have you thought of yourself as playing "second fiddle" to your leader? Why? Is it because of your own lack of understanding in how the Kingdom of God operates? Is it because of a poor self-image? Have others pigeon-holed you or treated you as inferior? Encourage yourself in the fact that God never sees you as a second fiddle. Be sure to forgive anyone who may have contributed to a negative self-image.

- In Romans 8:17, the apostle Paul even refers to us as *"joint-heirs **with Christ**"* (emphasis added). Ephesians 2:6 says that God has raised you up and you are seated with Christ in heavenly places. Does that sound like second fiddle to you? No, in Christ, we are all one. We simply fulfill different roles in the Body of Christ.

- Read in the Old Testament about Elisha and his relationship with Elijah, Aaron and his relationship with Moses (especially Exod. 17:11-13), and Joshua and his relationship with Moses. In the New Testament, read about Silas and Timothy and their individual relationships with the apostle Paul.

- Look up and meditate on verses that tell you who you are in Christ, and begin to see yourself as God sees you.

Dear God, there's no such thing as playing "second fiddle" in Your mind. Man has created such distinctions. I repent of giving place to any such thoughts and for minimizing my place in the Body of Christ. I believe that supporting my leader is what You've called me to do, and I'll serve You with gladness all the days of my life. Amen.

A WORD TO LEADERS
SEEKING A JOSHUA

REMEMBER, IT'S GOD'S MINISTRY

And masters, treat your servants considerately. Be fair with them. Don't forget for a minute that you, too, serve a Master—God in heaven (Colossians 4:1 TM).

Although this book has been written primarily for armorbearers, this and the next four devotions will be of particular interest to leaders. These principles are good for an armorbearer to understand as well, however, because he may already have people serving under him. Or perhaps God may appoint him to serve in the position of leader someday.

Joshua was never referred to in the Bible as Moses' armorbearer, but he was called Moses' minister in Joshua 1:1. The verb form of the word *minister* means: "to attend, to contribute to, to minister to, to wait on, and to serve." From this definition we see that Joshua's duty was to wait on Moses, to contribute to his success, and to serve him in everything he did. Had Moses had an armorbearer, it would have been Joshua because of their relationship.

Today apostles, prophets, evangelists, pastors, and teach-
ers all across our land are crying out, "Oh, God! Send me a
Joshua!" But are they willing to be a Moses to their Joshua?
If you are a leader, are you willing to make that investment
in your armorbearer? Now that puts the shoe on the other
foot.

Moses was willing to invest his anointing and his whole
life into Joshua. He was willing to relinquish control and
allow Joshua to take the people into the Promised Land,
even though Moses had personally shepherded the people
for 40 years in the wilderness. He knew that the children of
Israel belonged to God, not to him. He obeyed God when
He told him that Joshua would be the one to take the children of Israel into the Promised Land. (Deut. 32:48–52;
34:5,9.) Are you willing to do the same?

I am not saying that this is the situation for all leaders of
ministries, but the point I want to make is that *it's not the
leader's ministry.* If you are a leader reading this, *it's not your
ministry.* It's God's.

God is the One who places the vision in the spirit of a
leader. And when God starts something, He finishes it. The
work God has begun will continue long after the leader has
gone—if the leader has been willing to invest himself into
other people and if he has not allowed fear to keep him from
giving them the authority they have needed to help him.

May all of God's leaders remember that their ministry belongs to God, and may they invest generously in the lives of their armorbearers and all who follow them.

Developing the Spirit of a Leader

The following are signs of a leader worthy of a Joshua:

- He is secure in who he is and what God has called him to do.

- He is not afraid of his armorbearer or others trying to take over his position.

- He appreciates the time and effort his armorbearers and followers invest in serving him.

- He values others and recognizes the unique gifts that God has placed in them.

- He recognizes that he can't do all the work of the ministry himself.

- He is genuine and lavish with his praise.

- He rewards faithful service.

- He is kind toward and considerate of his armorbearer's personal life and relationship with his family.

Heavenly Father, thank You for giving me biblical examples of what a good leader is. I recognize that my ministry is not my own. It is Yours because it was Your idea and You put it into my heart. I will generously

invest time and resources into those You've called to help me, and I will pour my life into them. I will honor them as Your chosen vessels. Amen.

NOT NECESSARILY A BLOOD RELATIVE

For this reason I am sending to you Timothy, my son whom I love, who is faithful in the Lord. He will remind you of my way of life in Christ Jesus, which agrees with what I teach everywhere in every church (1 Corinthians 4:17 NIV).

If and when the time comes for you to seek a Joshua for your own ministry, pray for God's divinely appointed people to come your way, quality people who will carry your vision forward. I cannot stress the importance of this enough.

The people whom God sends may be in your own family, or they may not be. I once heard a minister say, "I would never let anybody but a member of the family run my ministry." That's a very strong statement—and totally *unscriptural.* The unity between a leader and his staff is in the spirit and not by blood.

Think about it. God raised up Joshua to assist Moses, not one of Moses' children. God raised up David and elected him to be king and not Saul's son Jonathan, the legal heir to the throne. God told Elijah to anoint Elisha as his successor, not one of Elijah's own family members. God anointed Samuel to be priest, not Eli's evil and wicked sons, Hophni and Phinehas. (1 Sam. 2:22–25.) We see a similar relationship in our New Testament text verse, which indicates that God raised up Timothy to assist Paul. In fact, Paul felt so close to Timothy that he referred to him as his own son whom he loved.

Now I will say that God may raise up your natural son or daughter to carry on your vision, but He could send someone else. The key is for you to do the will of God for your ministry no matter whom He may choose to help and succeed you.

Whatever kind of person you need, ask God for him. He will send you an associate, an executive assistant, a music director, an intercessor, a head usher, or whomever you may need or desire. Just begin to petition Him and start thanking Him for answering your prayer.

Developing the Spirit of a Leader

Note the following verses, especially the emphasized words that talk about our spiritual family—the family of God:

- *"When I think of the wisdom and scope of his plan, I fall down on my knees and pray to the Father of all the **great family of God**"* (Ephesians 3:14 TLB).

128

- *"And so we should not be like cringing, fearful slaves, but we should behave like **God's very own children, adopted into the bosom of his family,** and calling to him, 'Father, Father'"* (Romans 8:15 TLB).

- *"His unchanging plan has always been to adopt us **into his own family** by sending Jesus Christ to die for us. And he did this because he wanted to!"* (Ephesians 1:5 TLB).

- *"For Christ himself is our way of peace. He has made peace between us Jews and you Gentiles by **making us all one family**"* (Ephesians 2:14 TLB).

- *"Now you are no longer strangers to God and foreigners to heaven, but you are **members of God's very own family,** citizens of God's country, and you belong in God's household with every other Christian"* (Ephesians 2:19 TLB).

- *"All honor to God, the God and Father of our Lord Jesus Christ; for it is his boundless mercy that has given us the privilege of being born again so that we are now **members of God's own family**"* (1 Peter 1:3 TLB).

- *"And now this word to all of you: You should be like **one big happy family,** full of sympathy toward each other, loving one another with tender hearts and humble minds"* (1 Peter 3:8 TLB).

Father God, thank You for adopting me and my Christian brothers and sisters into Your family. Often I feel closer to my family in Christ than I do my own blood relatives. I receive whomever You send to assist me, whether they are my natural kin or my fellow believers. I love our Christian family of God. Amen.

DELEGATING AUTHORITY

And I will come down and talk with thee there: and I will take of the spirit which is upon thee, and will put it upon them; and they shall bear the burden of the people with thee, that thou bear it not thyself alone (Numbers 11:17).

In this verse, the Lord spoke to Moses about those He had chosen to assist him in leading the children of Israel. God took the spirit that He had put upon Moses and placed it upon the 70 elders. The purpose was so that these elders could function and minister to the people with the same love and anointing that Moses had operated. Numbers 11:24-25 describes the impartation:

And Moses went out, and told the people the words of the Lord, and gathered the seventy men of the elders of the people, and set them round about the tabernacle. And the Lord came down in a cloud, and spake unto him, and took of the spirit that was upon him, and gave it unto the seventy elders: and it came to pass, that, when the spirit rested upon them, they prophesied, and did not cease.

Jesus understood the importance of delegating authority. What would have happened if His attitude had been, "I am the leader here, and I don't have time to waste on you weak, faithless disciples"? This kind of attitude has been evident in some leaders, and it is of the devil, not God. The Lord has not called any of us to control the lives of other people, but to be an example to the flock.

God desires to send you quality people who can flow with you. But when you give them responsibility in an area, be big enough to give them the authority they need to carry out that responsibility. Sometimes leaders fear that they are losing control when others begin to grasp the vision and "run with it." That is when it is important for leaders to be secure in what God has called them to do. They must be confident that God has called these individuals to help them accomplish it.

Don't allow fear to keep you from allowing your staff to fully express their God-given creativity and gifts. A smart leader knows how to encourage and direct the talents and abilities of his people. This applies especially to armorbearers who have proven themselves faithful to bless you and help you minister to the people.

An official from Washington, D.C., shared an example with me of how he overcame a problem he had had with authority. He had liked the feeling of power it gave him when he was in charge. After becoming a Christian and being called to the pastorate, he said that it was still a struggle for him to delegate authority. In order to break this bondage, he began to "sow" authority into others. And in keeping with the biblical principle, you will find that, the more you give away, the more God will give back to you.

Developing the Spirit of a Leader

The following are some things that leaders can do to delegate and operate in biblical authority:

- Recognize that God is the One who assigned your staff to serve you.

- Refuse to be intimidated or fearful of losing control of your ministry.

- Provide a safe forum where your staff is encouraged to share their ideas, then respect those ideas.

- Seek the Lord about which ideas to implement, then give your staff the authority to execute them.

- Praise the staff for a job well done.

Heavenly Father, help me to have a correct understanding of biblical authority and delegation, and help me to implement Your principles with those under my supervision. I refuse to allow fear to rob me of the wealth of resources within them. Help me to recognize the unique

gifts and talents each possesses, and show me how I can encourage them to grow. Amen.

QUALIFICATIONS FOR ARMORBEARERS

Before they are asked to be deacons, they should be given other jobs in the church as a test of their character and ability, and if they do well, then they may be chosen as deacons (1 Timothy 3:10 TLB).

Leaders should look for people who possess the spirit of an armorbearer. And those who feel called to be an armorbearer should strive to be worthy of that calling. Here are some guidelines:

- Do they have a disciplined prayer life?
- Are they grounded in the Word?
- Are they faithful to the church?
- Is their family intact?
- Do they tithe?
- Are you at ease in their presence?
- Are they at ease in your presence?

- Are they genuinely interested in people of all types and races?

- Do they possess a strong and steady will?

- Do they avoid murmuring and complaining?

- Are they optimistic?

- Do they submit to authority?

- Are they good listeners?

- Are they disciplined, both mentally and physically?

- Are they loyal?

- Are they temperate and not given to alcohol, drugs, tobacco, or anything else that would harm them?

- Are they strong in their love walk, or do they give place to anger or strife?

- Can they keep confidences?

Although these guidelines are mentioned to help leaders recognize and choose capable armorbearers, they are also the signs of mature believers and leaders. They are qualities we all should aspire to.

Developing the Spirit of a Leader

The Bible has quite a bit to say about the qualifications for being an armorbearer:

- *"Likewise must the deacons be grave, not doubletongued, not given to much wine, not greedy of filthy lucre; holding the mystery of the faith in a pure conscience. And let these also first be proved; then let them use the office of a deacon, being found blameless. Even so must their wives be grave, not slanderers, sober, faithful in all things. Let the deacons be the husbands of one wife, ruling their children and their own houses well"* (1 Timothy 3:8-12).

- *"A bishop then must be blameless, the husband of one wife, vigilant, sober, of good behavior, given to hospitality, apt to teach; not given to wine, no striker, not greedy of filthy lucre; but patient, not a brawler, not covetous; one that ruleth well his own house, having his children in subjection with all gravity; (For if a man know not how to rule his own house, how shall he take care of the church of God?) Not a novice, lest being lifted up with pride he fall into the condemnation of the devil. Moreover he must have a good report of them which are without; lest he fall into reproach and the snare of the devil"* (1 Timothy 3:2-7).

- *"For a bishop must be blameless, as the steward of God; not self-willed, not soon angry, not given to wine, no striker, not given to filthy lucre; but a lover of hospitality, a lover of good men, sober, just, holy, temperate; holding fast the faithful word as he hath been taught, that he may be able by sound doctrine both to exhort and to convince the gainsayers"* (Titus 1:7-9).

Father, You know what it takes to serve as an effective armorbearer, and I thank You for giving us these guidelines. Now armorbearers can know what is required of them, and leaders can know what to look for and expect in their armorbearers. It will help us do all things decently and in order. Help me to fulfill my role with excellence and to follow these guidelines in my own life. Amen.

DEVELOPING THE SPIRIT
OF AN ARMORBEARER

FREEING YOURSELF
FROM PRIDE & ANGER

Love is patient, love is kind. It does not envy, it does not boast, it is not proud. It is not rude, it is not self-seeking, it is not easily angered, it keeps no record of wrongs (1 Corinthians 13:4-5 NIV).

Every child of God—from leaders on down—needs to develop the character of an armorbearer, because the character of an armorbearer is the character of Christ. I believe the Church really needs teaching in this area right now. We have learned a lot about faith, prosperity, healing, and intercession, but I feel we must place more emphasis on character development. God's power is hindered when we walk after the flesh and not by the spirit. People get hurt and the ministry suffers.

I would like to share some steps that I believe will be beneficial to follow in your effort to develop the spirit of a true God-called armorbearer.

Step 1. Free yourself from pride. Evidences of pride include:

- an independent spirit (refusal to look to God or others for help),

- failure to admit mistakes,

- a lack of a teachable spirit,

- a rebellious attitude toward those in authority,

- a proud countenance,

- self-centered conversation,

- intolerance toward the mistakes of others, and

- a bossy attitude.

Step 2: Free yourself from anger. Evidences of anger include:

- temper tantrums (at any age);

- an angry reaction to supposed injustice;

- expressed frustration over unchangeable circumstances;

- grumbling, murmuring, and complaining; and

- extreme sensitivity and touchiness.

Pride and anger have no place in your life as an armorbearer, but the antidote is the love of God, which is shed abroad in your heart (Rom. 5:5). Make a quality decision to grow in humility and love and godly character. Then you will be developing the true spirit of an armorbearer.

Developing the Spirit of an Armorbearer

* Look up and study the following verses to see what God has to say about pride and anger: James 1:20; James 4:6,10; Proverbs 13:10; Proverbs 14:17; Proverbs 16:18,32; Proverbs 22:24-25; and Proverbs 29:23.

* Everyone deals with pride and anger on some level, but if it seems to be a stronghold in your life, ask God to reveal the root cause.

  * Do you suffer from self-hatred or a poor self-image?

  * Did you grow up in a shame-based home?

  * Were you criticized or expected to be perfect?

  * Are you performance oriented? Do you hide behind your works?

  * On some level do you believe God expects you to be perfect and that it is not okay to make mistakes?

  * Have you suffered a tremendous injustice?

  * Ask the Holy Spirit to expose any other contributing factors.

  * If you answered yes to any of these, I encourage you to meditate on verses about God's great love

and acceptance of you—even when you fail. Ask God to heal your wounds. You don't have to hide behind your performance with Him. He appreciates what you do, but He loves you because you are you.

Father, I repent of any pride or anger that I have given place to, for they are so opposite of the character of Christ. Since I am Your child, they have no place in me. There may be factors that have contributed to my tendency to be proud or angry, but I ask that Your love flush them out from the roots and heal any wounds in my soul. Help me to walk in Your love, which is patient, kind, and doesn't think more highly of itself than it ought. Heal anyone I have hurt, and love others through me. Amen.

FREEING YOURSELF FROM
IMMORALITY & BITTERNESS

The acts of the sinful nature are obvious: sexual immorality, impurity and debauchery; idolatry and witchcraft; hatred, discord, jealousy, fits of rage, selfish ambition, dissensions, factions and envy; drunkenness, orgies, and the like. I warn you, as I did before, that those who live like this will not inherit the kingdom of God (Galatians 5:19-21 NIV).

In the previous devotion, we discussed the importance of developing the character of Christ if a person is to become a true armorbearer. Two other traits that have infiltrated the Church and must be overcome are immorality and bitterness. Armorbearers—as well as all believers—have been set apart to live holy lives, free from the filth of the world. And with the love of God in our hearts—the love that forgives—bitterness certainly has no place. How can we be the light of the world if our lives are full of darkness?

Step 3: Free yourself from immorality. Evidences of a spirit of impurity include:

- sensual conversation,

- the reading of impure materials,

- an impure attitude and improper actions toward members of the opposite sex or the same sex,

- a desire to listen to sensual music,

- sensual dress or appearance, and

- carnal curiosity.

Step 4: Free yourself from bitterness. Evidences of a spirit of bitterness include:

- sarcastic and critical talk,

- an inability to trust people,

- frequent illness,

- self-pity, and

- a sad countenance.

These are all areas in which we need to judge ourselves in order to break satan's power in our lives, to be pleasing to God, and to be true armorbearers. This will be accomplished as we lead lives above reproach, giving ourselves totally and freely for one another, carrying the shield for our brothers and sisters, and joining our faith together. If we will do that, we will truly become God's great army. We will go forth to conquer in the power of the Holy Spirit.

Developing the Spirit of an Armorbearer

The following verses provide some food for thought and meditation:

- *"Having therefore these promises, dearly beloved, let us cleanse ourselves from all filthiness of the flesh and spirit, perfecting holiness in the fear of God"* (2 Corinthians 7:1).

- *"Just as you used to be slaves to all kinds of sin, so now you must let yourselves be slaves to all that is right and holy"* (Romans 6:19 TLB).

- *"And that ye put on the new man, which after God is created in righteousness and true holiness"* (Ephesians 4:24).

- *"For God hath not called us unto uncleanness, but unto holiness"* (1 Thessalonians 4:7).

- *"Looking diligently lest any man fail of the grace of God; lest any root of bitterness springing up trouble you, and thereby many be defiled"* (Hebrews 12:15).

- *"Let all bitterness, and wrath, and anger, and clamor, and evil speaking, be put away from you, with all malice: And be ye kind one to another, tenderhearted, forgiving one another, even as God for Christ's sake hath forgiven you"* (Ephesians 4:31-32).

Heavenly Father, I repent of any impure and sensual thoughts and actions, and I thank You for cleansing me from all unrighteousness. I choose to live a holy and godly life that will be a light in this dark world. I also repent of any bitterness I've harbored. I choose to forgive and release anyone who has hurt me or wronged me. Thank You for Your love that heals my wounds and sets me free. Amen.

RECOGNIZING THE HUMAN SIDE OF A LEADER

REMAINING LOYAL NO MATTER WHAT

Two are better than one; because they have a good reward for their labor. For if they fall, the one will lift up his fellow: but woe to him that is alone when he falleth; for he hath not another to help him up (Ecclesiastes 4:9-10).

In your life of service to your leader, you will discover that he has a very human side as well as being an anointed man of God. A good example of this is the relationship between Elisha and Elijah.

Historians tell us that Elisha served Elijah for 15 to 20 years, during which time Elisha heard everything that Elijah said and saw everything he did, whether good or bad. He was with him under all kinds of circumstances.

You may remember the story of when King Ahab's son, Ahaziah, sent soldiers after Elijah. At one point, Elijah cried out to the captain of the guard, *"If I be a man of God, then let fire come down from heaven, and consume thee and thy fifty"* (2 Kings 1:10). The fire fell, and 50 men died, leaving 50 horses to go running back to town with empty saddles.

How would you have responded if you had been Elijah's associate? You would have thought to yourself, *Boy, am I glad I'm on his side!* You would have been proud to tell everyone, "I work for Elijah."

Then there is the story of the famous contest on Mount Carmel between Elijah and the heathen prophets to prove which was the true God: Jehovah or Baal. After the Lord had sent fire from Heaven to consume the sacrifice, His prophet Elijah took a sword and slew the 400 prophets of Baal.

Following an experience like that, you would think that this man would not be afraid of anything. But when the wicked Queen Jezebel sent a message threatening the life of Elijah, he became frightened and fled into the wilderness (1 Kings 19:1–4).

How do you respond when your leader reacts in fear, when you discover that he is human just as you are? Have you seen him fall, make a great mistake, or even get into sin? What's your reaction? Are you ready to leave and find some other place of employment, or are you willing to help, support, and see him restored? Here is where we really find out what we are made of.

If there is a true attitude of repentance, a faithful man will stand with his leader. A true armorbearer will control his tongue in public, but he will also speak boldly in private prayer. A true armorbearer will be loyal through thick and thin. Are you up to the challenge?

Developing the Spirit of an Armorbearer

First of all, it is vital that you support your leader in prayer, to help him overcome pitfalls before he ever comes near them. But in the event that your leader falls, a true armorbearer will do several things:

- Instead of believing rumors, he will go to his leader to discuss the matter.

- He will not react in shock or anger, but he will calmly listen to what his leader has to say.

- *"A talebearer revealeth secrets: but he that is of a faithful spirit concealeth the matter"* (Prov. 11:13). A true armorbearer will not be guilty of spreading gossip or airing "dirty laundry."

- He will forgive.

- He will verbalize his forgiveness, commitment, and support to his leader.

- He will stand stalwart until there is total restoration.

Dear God, I am committed to living a life of faithful service to my leader. Because You have called me to be close by his side, I will see him under all sorts of circumstances, both good and bad. I will witness his victories, and I will witness his shortcomings and failures. If he ever falls, I pray that You will help me to work through the situation so that I can stand by his side until he is

restored. I am committed to being faithful and true through thick and thin. Amen.

THE FOUR FACES

And the first beast was like a lion, and the second beast like a calf, and the third beast had a face as a man, and the fourth was like a flying eagle (Revelation 4:7).

In this verse we see the four faces of Jesus: a lion, a calf, a man, and an eagle. We see Jesus as a lion in dealing with the devil and sin. We see Him as a calf as He came to serve humanity. We see Him as a man as He held the little children and blessed them. And we see Him as an eagle as He prayed, preached, and healed the people.

In every leader you will see a lion when it comes to dealing with a problem, a calf when it comes to serving people, a man when it comes to tending the sheep, and an eagle when it comes to standing up to minister the Word of the Lord. But you will also see your leader as a man when he is hurt and wounded.

Most people only see their leader as an eagle, but as his armorbearer you will see all four faces of your leader. You will see him when he is less than full of faith and power, when he says something or does something that may offend you, when things are tight financially and you have to cut back the budget of your department.

It is easy to respect your leader when he is functioning as an eagle under God's anointing. But you must also respect him when times are hard and he is operating more as a man. Respect is due the leader no matter how he may appear or feel.

Some people have the mistaken idea that those who work in the ministry sit around all day praying and fellow-shipping with one another. The ministry, however, is *work, work,* and more *work*. It requires an ability to work with other people without giving or taking offense. True armor-bearing is the ability to see the human side of our leaders and still maintain respect for them.

Developing the Spirit of an Armorbearer

The following are some ways that you can show respect for your leader under all circumstances:

- Respect is a choice. Respect your leader as a man, a minister, a father, etc.

- Always refer to your leader by his title and not his first name alone. For example: Pastor John, Brother Roberts, Reverend Graham, Dr. Smith, etc.

- Always be on time—or better yet, early—for appointments with him, and make yourself available 24/7.

- Maintain the boundary between your two positions. Your leader may relax the boundary on his end; he may confide in you, ask you for advice, or pour out his heart to you; but you must still maintain the line of respect and not become lax. Maintain excellence and keep a sharp edge.

- When you see your leader struggling, pray. Ask the Lord to show you ways that you can be an encouragement. No matter what, stay positive and strong in faith.

- Recognize and be able to distinguish between your leader's four faces. Because of your close working relationship, you will see a side of your leader that few others see. You will see how he interacts with his wife and children, how he handles challenges with them. What you observe in private should stay private so that your leader can feel at ease enough to allow you into his personal domain.

Heavenly Father, the man I serve is such a mighty man of God, and it is a privilege to serve under one so anointed in ministry. I do realize, however, that he is human. Help me be able to separate his anointing and ministry office from the natural, everyday man. I will keep a guard over my mouth and maintain all

confidences, keeping private matters private. Help me to be worthy of his confidence and not to ever do anything that would violate the level of trust we have developed. Cause it to grow stronger every day. Amen.

RECOGNIZING THE RIGHT
OF DIVINE AUTHORITY

*Jesus said, "Father, if it is Your will, take this cup away
from Me; nevertheless not My will, but Yours, be done"*
(Luke 22:42 NKJV).

U nderstanding the right of divine authority is another
thing we must come to understand in order to be true
armorbearers. We must know, recognize, and yield to
God's authority in our lives. We have to pray daily, "Father,
not my will, but Yours be done." We have to be determined
in our hearts to stay in God's will regardless of the cost or
consequences.

When we look at Jesus, we might think that because He
was the Son of God He had no problem at all in fulfilling
God's will for His life. Let's look at Hebrews 5:7–8 to see if
this is true:

*Who in the days of his flesh, when he had offered up
prayers and supplications with strong crying and tears*

unto him that was able to save him from death, and was heard in that he feared; though he were a Son, yet learned he obedience by the things which he suffered.

We see Jesus in "strong crying and tears" before the Father, yet choosing to remain in God's will and praying to fulfill the divine call that was upon Him.

Whatever it takes, whether you are happy or hurting, whether things are going smoothly or they're very hard, make a firm commitment in your heart to fulfill God's plan for your life.

Several years ago, the Lord said something to me that has helped me during hard times. He said, *Keep your eyes on the resurrection, and you can endure the Cross.* The Cross is not a burden; it's the call of God on our lives. If it is God's will for you to stay in one place for the rest of your life in order to give yourself to and for someone else, then let God's will be done. It's not always easy, but obeying God always pays.

Developing the Spirit of an Armorbearer

Let the following verses encourage you:

- *"Then Peter and the other apostles answered and said, We ought to obey God rather than men"* (Acts 5:29).

- *"If ye be willing and obedient, ye shall eat the good of the land"* (Isaiah 1:19).

- *"Behold, to obey is better than sacrifice, and to hearken than the fat of rams. For rebellion is as the sin of witchcraft, and stubbornness is as iniquity and idolatry"* (1 Samuel 15:22-23).

- *"For I know the plans I have for you, says the Lord. They are plans for good and not for evil, to give you a future and a hope"* (Jeremiah 29:11 TLB).

- *"For God is at work within you, helping you want to obey him, and then helping you do what he wants"* (Philippians 2:13 TLB).

Dear God, I'm glad You are a good God and that I can trust You with my life. It's not always easy to obey, but I am committed to follow Jesus' example and submit to Your will. Whether it is Your plan for me to stay in my current position for the rest of my life or You have plans to put me into an entirely different position, I choose to follow You and serve You with gladness. Thank You for working in me to will and do of Your good pleasure, for when I am willing and obedient, I will eat the good of the land. Amen.

BECOMING PREGNANT
WITH THE VISION

Sow to yourselves in righteousness, reap in mercy; break up your fallow ground: for it is time to seek the Lord, till he come and rain righteousness upon you (Hosea 10:12).

One day I was thinking about what God had placed in my heart to do for Him. I had—and still do have—a God-ordained desire to see churches and Bible schools raised up in all nations around the world. Many years ago, I asked the Lord, "Father, how is this vision going to ever come into reality?"

He said to me, *Son, you are going to have to bring it forth by intimacy, pregnancy, travail, and birth.*

This made everything very clear to me. Spiritual birth takes place in much the same way that natural birth occurs. In order to bring forth in the spiritual realm, we must become intimate with God. I believe that today the Holy Spirit is speaking the words of our text to the Body of

Christ: To become intimate with the Lord, we must seek Him with our whole heart. From that intimacy comes pregnancy.

From pregnancy will eventually come travail. *To travail* means "to intercede, care for, pray, and speak God's Word over that vision or plan." Then, finally, we must give birth to the fulfillment of God's will in our lives. It will not drop down on us out of the sky, however. We must draw near to God, but when we do, He will draw near to us (James 4:8).

Developing the Spirit of an Armorbearer

If you want to develop an intimate relationship with God, nothing can take the place of simply spending time with Him. Has your relationship become stale? Try doing something different.

- Take your Bible and a notebook to a park or some other location other than home. Treat it like a date. Away from home, there won't be the distractions of the TV, telephone (turn off that cell phone!), bills to pay, etc. You could sit in your car or find a quiet nook in a library. Or dedicate a room in your home to be your sanctuary. The place is unimportant. What is important is that you set aside time for Him away from distractions.

- You can simply sit still while soaking in His presence. Just be with Him. Have you ever noticed that with people you are close to, you don't always have to be talking to each other to enjoy one another's company?

- Pray in the Spirit. This will build up your spirit, and oftentimes you will sense the interpretation flowing along with it.

- Find a private place and sing, praise, and worship your Father.

- Ask God to lead you as you read your Bible. You can read a lot or simply meditate on a verse that you feel drawn to.

- Listen. Don't be uncomfortable in the silence. God has things to say to you, but your mind must be quiet enough to hear.

- Write down your thoughts and any revelation that comes during your intimate time with God.

Father God, relationship is what You are all about. It was one of the reasons You sent Jesus to us, so that we could relate to You. I ask You to forgive me for being so busy that it has taken away from my time with You. My heart yearns for intimacy with You, and Your Word says You yearn to be with me too. I know You are knocking on the door of my heart, so I open it to You. Come on in and let us share a spiritual meal together. As our hearts are knit together, I know You'll impregnate me with the vision You have for my life. Help me

*to nurture it in prayer as it grows. With Your help, I
know I will eventually give birth to it. Amen.*

THE BIRTH OF A VISION REQUIRES TRAVAIL

Likewise the Spirit also helpeth our infirmities: for we know not what we should pray for as we ought: but the Spirit itself maketh intercession for us with groanings which cannot be uttered. And he that searcheth the hearts knoweth what is the mind of the Spirit, because he maketh intercession for the saints according to the will of God (Romans 8:26-27).

Once we have developed an intimate relationship with God and become pregnant with a dream or a vision planted in us by Him, then we must begin to nurture that vision, causing it to grow and develop.

Some of the most miserable people in this world are women who are pregnant and overdue. They know the birth is inevitable, but they don't know when it will take place. They feel uncomfortable, like they will pop if the child doesn't come forth. Likewise, it is quite uncomfortable for those Christians in the world who are "pregnant" with a vision from God and yet have not been able to give birth to that vision. Sooner or later it will lead to godly travail, without which there can be no birth. That travail is our intercession. Intercession is a prayer that goes before God for someone else. It is praying that God's will be done for others. As you commit to this kind of prayer you will discover that it will be easier to work with your leaders. As you pray for others you will sense God's love being poured through you for them. In this the law of giving and receiving will work for you. What you make happen for someone else, God makes happen for you. Isaiah 40:3 (NLT) states, *"Listen! I hear the voice of someone shouting, 'Make a highway for the Lord through the wilderness. Make a straight, smooth road through the desert for our God.'"* John the Baptist was the forerunner of Jesus. He prepared the way for Jesus' first coming. You and I are preparing the way for the Lord's second coming.

One day the Lord revealed Isaiah 40:3 to me in this way: "The voice of someone is shouting in Little Rock, Arkansas, 'Prepare ye the way of the Lord, make straight in Little Rock a highway for our God.'"

Intercession is like building a highway for the Lord. We have to do the work first, but then God will send His glory. If we will be patient and faithful—if we will follow the process of intimacy, pregnancy, travail, and birth—we will see the fulfillment of our heavenly dreams and visions.

Developing the Spirit of an Armorbearer

- During the time that you are pregnant with the vision, when you have done all to stand and you are awaiting delivery, make good use of your time. Continue interceding according to God's Word, but also use the time to prepare. A woman who is pregnant with her first child usually reads everything she can get her hands on having to do with parenting. In the same way, while you are in the waiting mode, search out as many resources as possible that have to do with your vision.

- If your vision is to go on the mission field, for example, read the many testimonies of others who have gone before you. Learn what worked for them and what didn't. Correspond or meet with other missionaries. Take a language course, learn about the culture, maybe even take a trip to the place you desire to go to long term. Intercede for the country that is on your heart.

- There are numerous things you can do to prepare for the inevitable birth of your calling. Make the most of this time, because when this season is over and you are fulfilling the vision God has for you, you may be so busy that you won't have time to work on foundational things. Build the foundation now and bathe it in prayer.

- The following are some verses you can meditate on for encouragement: Habakkuk 2:2-3; Romans 8:34; Hebrews 7:25; Hebrews 10:36; Proverbs 13:12; Second Timothy 2:15; and 1 Corinthians 10:4.

Dear God, I am indeed pregnant with the vision You have planted within me. Sometimes I get so excited that I could just pop. Other times I get discouraged because where I am is uncomfortable and it seems like I will never give birth to my dream. But because Your Word has promised that it will come forth, I will be faithful to continue interceding and preparing the way of the Lord. Amen.

FOLLOWING GOD'S
PREDETERMINED COURSE

*Being predestinated according to the purpose of him
who worketh all things after the counsel of his own will*
(Ephesians 1:11).

The word translated "predestinated" in this verse means
"predetermined."[1] God has a predetermined, pre-
designed course for every one of us. That course was set
before we were ever born into this earth.

The Lord has said to each of us: *"Before I formed thee in
the belly I knew thee"* (Jer. 1:5). God knew you and me
before the foundation of the world, and He set an individual course for each of us to follow. Now it is up to you and
me to discover God's course for us and to follow that course
so that we may give spiritual birth to the dream and vision
He has had in mind for us.

Be faithful where you are right now, and determine to
stay in God's will so that every promise in God's Word can

be fulfilled in your life. The apostle Paul said, "I have fought a good fight, I have finished my course" (2 Tim. 4:7). Paul fought to stay on course, and he made it. He finished the course laid out for him by God. Discover what your course is, and then stay with it and never give up until you have reached your God-ordained destination and goal.

Developing the Spirit of an Armorbearer

- Have you ever been on a road trip and gotten off course? Perhaps you tried a shortcut that, as it turned out, actually took you longer to get there. Or has anyone ever told you about a shortcut that really did work? A course that was off the beaten path? We can draw some beneficial parallels from this in regard to following God's course for our lives.

- You may know your ultimate destination now, but you need guidance on how to get there. First and foremost, God's Word is a lamp for your feet and a light for your path (Ps. 119:105). And because it is God's predetermined plan for you, He sees the big picture. He can see the shortcuts and pitfalls, and He's given you the Holy Spirit to lead you and guide you. You needn't look to external guidance because the Holy Spirit lives inside you, and it is from within that you'll get the inside track.

- Meditate on the following verses to encourage you on your journey. Make them personal prayers and confessions for your individual situation:

"For we are his workmanship, created in Christ Jesus unto good works, which God hath before ordained that we should walk in them" (Ephesians 2:10).

"I press toward the mark for the prize of the high calling of God in Christ Jesus" (Philippians 3:14).

"The steps of a good man are ordered by the Lord: and he delighteth in his way" (Psalm 37:23).

"Thou hast enlarged my steps under me, that my feet did not slip" (Psalm 18:36).

"In all thy ways acknowledge him, and he shall direct thy paths" (Proverbs 3:6).

"And thine ears shall hear a word behind thee, saying, This is the way, walk ye in it, when ye turn to the right hand, and when ye turn to the left" (Isaiah 30:21).

"But none of these things move me, neither count I my life dear unto myself, so that I might finish my course with joy, and the ministry, which I have received of the Lord Jesus, to testify the gospel of the grace of God" (Acts 20:24).

Father, knowing that You had me in mind when You created the earth is an awesome thought. Even then,

You set forth a specific course for me to follow, one I have been uniquely and intricately designed for. I am committed to following Your path for me, and I trust You to lead and guide me so that I can stay on course. I won't try to find a shortcut, but like Paul, I will press toward the mark until I finish the race. Your joy shall be my strength. Amen.

Endnote

1. *The Merriam-Webster Dictionary*, 1998, s.v. "predestinated."

APPRECIATE YOUR GIFT

But now hath God set the members every one of them in the body, as it hath pleased him (1 Corinthians 12:18).

The fulfillment of the predetermined course God has set for you is dependent on the proper use of the divine gifts that have been bestowed on you.

Every year my family gets together on Christmas Eve. Because my family is so large, prior to Christmas we draw names to see whom we will buy presents for. One Christmas, while handing out the gifts, I noticed that my twin brother had received two presents. His name had accidentally been placed on two different gifts. When I opened my present, I was disappointed in what I received. I then looked at my twin brother and the two nice gifts he had. Later, sensing my disappointment, my wife came over to console me.

"Don't worry, Terry," she said, "when we get back home, we will exchange it for something you like better."

Now the very same thing happens in the Body of Christ. We open the gifts God has given us, and we run to someone else to see what he has received. Then we hurry to another to see what gift he has been given. When we look at our gift from the Lord, we are unhappy with it and immediately think to ourselves, *I know what I'll do; I'll swap it for something I like better.*

This is why there are so many people running around in church circles today claiming to be an apostle or a prophet or a teacher. Many times what they are really doing is "gift swapping," because they do not like the spiritual gift that God has bestowed upon them.

You had absolutely nothing to do with choosing the gifts that God has placed inside you. He bestows gifts according to His will, and it is up to you to receive the gift He's given you and allow Him to add more gifts *"as He wills"* (1 Cor. 12:11).

Developing the Spirit of an Armorbearer

- For a person to really understand his gifts and how to flow in them sometimes takes many years. First, you must recognize the gift God has given you. If you don't know what it is, there are excellent Christian books and courses designed to help you discover it.

- Be thankful. A gift is a good thing. If you are coveting someone else's gift, examine your heart as to why.

And talk to your Father God. Ask Him to show you how your gift can be fully utilized to bless as many people as possible.

• Meditate on what God has to say about gifts. In addition to the ones below, also read Romans 12:4-8 and First Corinthians 12:1-12.

"For the gifts and calling of God are without repentance" (Romans 11:29).

"A man's gift maketh room for him, and bringeth him before great men" (Proverbs 18:16).

"God has given each of us the ability to do certain things well" (Romans 12:6 TLB).

"For I would that all men were even as I myself. But every man hath his proper gift of God, one after this manner, and another after that" (1 Corinthians 7:7).

"For the body is not one member, but many. If the foot shall say, Because I am not the hand, I am not of the body; is it therefore not of the body? And if the ear shall say, Because I am not the eye, I am not of the body; is it therefore not of the body? If the whole body were an eye, where were the hearing? If the whole were hearing, where were the smelling? But now hath God set the members every one of them in the body, as it hath pleased him" (1 Corinthians 12:14-18).

Dear God, thank You for the gifts You've given me. Help me to recognize them, and provide me with opportunities to put them into practice. I ask You to forgive me for the times I've taken my gift for granted and coveted others' gifts. I rejoice in my gift now and ask You to help me use it to bless many. Amen.

GOD'S THE ONE
WHO WILL EXALT YOU

For promotion cometh neither from the east, nor from the west, nor from the south. But God is the judge: he putteth down one, and setteth up another (Psalm 75:6).

We've stated many times throughout this book that as you are faithful in the small things, God will make you a ruler over many. As we stay with the assignment and the gifts God has given each of us, He will bring our gift before great men (Prov. 18:16). This may not happen overnight, but God always fulfills His promises. When it doesn't seem like anything is happening and that you will always be serving in the background, your Father sees you and will reward your faithfulness.

I remember one day while attending Bible school, I saw a fellow I knew come into class all dressed up. This was unusual because he generally wore jeans. When I asked him why he was so dressed up, he answered, "Because all the big shots from the denominational headquarters are coming to school today; just stick with me and I'll introduce you to the really big ones."

I was so grieved in my heart that I went to my room and told the Lord that if that was how the ministry worked, then He could count me out.

The Lord said so clearly to me that day, *Son, don't you realize that you have already been introduced to the Big One?*

That's right. They don't come any "bigger" than God, and you don't have to play any games to gain His attention. Stay with your individual assignment, and in due time He will exalt you.

Developing the Spirit of an Armorbearer

The following are some examples of God exalting ordinary individuals to a place of honor. None exalted themselves, but God saw their hearts, and in due season they reaped the rewards of their faithfulness.

- Rebekah was drawing water from a well and with a servant's heart offered a drink to Abraham's servant and his camels. She went on to marry Isaac, a very wealthy man. Together they bore Jacob, who was in the lineage of Jesus (Matt. 1:2).

- David was just a shepherd boy being faithful in his work when he was anointed to be king. The Lord specifically told Samuel not to look on his appearance, for He saw David's heart (1 Sam. 16:6-13). He, too, was part of the lineage of Jesus.

- Ruth gave up her life in her homeland to follow her mother-in-law after the death of their husbands. She went on to marry Boaz. Together they, too, bore a son in the lineage of Jesus (Matt. 1:5). The Book of Ruth in the Bible tells her story.

- Esther was an ordinary woman who had favor with the king and went on to marry him. She saved her people from death, and a book of the Bible was written to tell her story.

- Mary was another ordinary woman who found great favor with God. She bore the Savior.

These are just a few of the many examples of ordinary but faithful individuals who did not promote themselves but were highly exalted by God.

Dear God, I feel like I'm just an ordinary, everyday sort of person, just being faithful to do the small things in Your Kingdom. I see how others have set out to promote themselves, oftentimes hurting others in the process, but I refuse to get into the political game. You see my heart, You know what I do, and I trust You for any promotion that comes. Even if I am never exalted in a public way,

I thank You that You will reward me for being faithful to Your work. Amen.

TEND TO YOUR
PRESENT ASSIGNMENT

Jesus said, "Well done, good and faithful servant; you were faithful over a few things, I will make you ruler over many things" (Matthew 25:21 NKJV).

There was a time when I saw God begin to do many great things in my life. It was a time of the manifestation and fulfillment of many dreams and visions. During this period, I started experiencing more problems and having more frequent confrontations than ever before. As director of our Bible and mission school, I felt like a fireman. As soon as one "blaze" was extinguished, another would crop up somewhere else.

On one hand, God was doing great things, but on the other hand I felt run down and discouraged. At this time I thought to myself, *I will just let my wife* (who was the administrator of the school) *start doing more; I'll go to the mission field where the work is fun and I can just send back postcards.*

My mind was made up to do that until, while in prayer, I saw in my spirit a vision of David being anointed by Samuel to be king. The Lord asked me, *What did David do after he was anointed king?*

I thought for a moment and answered, "He went back to tending his father's sheep."

The Lord continued, *Had David gone out looking for a giant to kill at that time, the lion and the bear would have eaten his flock. The school is your flock, so you had better tend to it.*

"Yes, Sir," I said. "I see that very clearly."

Whether you are a pastor, an associate pastor, a music director, or a layman, each of us has a flock. That flock belongs to us individually, and God expects us to tend it. David's flock was his assignment from God, and he knew that. Although he had been anointed to be king of Israel, his first priority at the moment was to continue to tend to his first assignment. I knew that if I did not take the time to invest myself into the students under my care, I could not expect them to flow with me once they had reached the mission field.

The giants will come. And if you will stay with your assignment, at just the right time, you will meet and conquer your giant just as David met and overcame his. Like

David, you will be exalted—*after* you have first proven yourself faithful.

You may look at your current condition and position and wonder how God could ever use you. You may think to yourself, *I am not the person in charge, so I have to stay submitted to other people. How will I ever get to fulfill my own dream and vision?*

Be at peace and know that God's Word is not written for leaders only. It is written for the Body of Christ, and that includes you—God's armorbearer—right where you are today.

Developing the Spirit of an Armorbearer

- Who or what is your flock at the moment? Whomever or whatever it is, it is where God needs you now.

- Let the Scriptures below encourage you. In the last two examples, the individuals being written to were already in leadership positions of oversight, but the principle is still the same: don't get in a hurry for the next phase of ministry. Serve your current flock well today. Let these verses minister to you: Ecclesiastes 3:1; Psalm 31:15; Acts 20:28; and First Peter 5:2-4.

Father God, thank You for the "flock" You've given me. My heart is so full of the vision You've put inside me that sometimes it is hard to give my current assignment

my full attention. I repent of that. If I'm constantly living in the future, there is no way I can be truly faithful where I am now. I recommit myself to the position You have me in now. My times are in Your hands, Father, and I trust You to orchestrate my life as it pleases You. Amen.

IT PAYS TO OBEY

He hath made every thing beautiful in his time (Ecclesiastes 3:11).

Years ago I was in Austria and was talking with a national pastor who shared something that blessed me greatly.

In 1987, when I was in that country, I was scheduled to lead a Bible conference. I struggled within myself as to what to teach. I rose up early the day before the conference and said to the Lord, "Father, what do You want me to teach?" I had not consulted with Him about His direction.

The Lord said, *Preach on the pattern of the New Testament Church.*

I began reading through the Book of Acts to discover what that pattern was. The theme of all the messages I received was this: If Austria is going to be won to God, it must be done through the local church.

I realized then that God was saying, *Today is the day of the local church in Austria.* I believe that is true of the whole world.

This Austrian pastor shared with me how as a result of that one conference, four local churches had been started in four different areas. I was so blessed and moved in my heart that God had used me to affect a nation. It had happened because I was obedient and taught what He wanted taught.

In 1989, we opened the first Full Gospel Bible school in the history of that European nation. I have found God to be so faithful to us as we determine to *walk in our anointing, stay in submission to His divine authority,* and *fulfill our God-ordained assignment.* It takes an understanding of all these areas to be an armorbearer.

Developing the Spirit of an Armorbearer

Let's take a look at the three principles just mentioned:

- Walk in your anointing. Do you know what that is? What about you just seems to flow, almost effortlessly? It shouldn't be something you have to work up. It's a gift that God has given you.

- Stay in submission to His divine authority. Do you know what God wants you to be doing right now? If not, are you willing to repent and get back in the game? Are you willing to stay in the place God has you until He releases you to do something else?

- Fulfill your God-ordained assignment. Sooner or later, if you will remain faithful and submit to God's leading, you will fulfill your God-ordained assignment. It will be a day of great rejoicing, and many will be blessed.

Heavenly Father, the very fact that the Holy Spirit lives in me is testament to the fact that Your anointing is in me. Help me recognize the gifts You've put in me, and teach me how to flow in them to bless others. I am committed to stay when You say stay and go when You say go. You are truly the Lord of my life and all that I do. Finally, I trust You to move me into position at just the right time so that I may fulfill the assignment You've ordained for me from the beginning. Amen.

REEVALUATE YOUR LIFE AND MINISTRY

Except the Lord build the house, they labor in vain that build it: except the Lord keep the city, the watchman waketh but in vain (Psalm 127:1).

Ours could very well be the generation that rises to meet Jesus in the air. It is time for us to reevaluate our lives and our ministries to make sure that we are where we need to be and that we are doing what we need to be doing. Satan does not mind it when we build our dreams and visions, as long as he is the head contractor. If what we are doing is not of the Spirit and directed by Him, any edifice we erect is going to fall. In fact, satan will allow us to build, making sure that we smear God's name all over our own dreams and visions so that when they fail, it will appear that God has failed.

When you set out to build the Kingdom, you must be sure that God is 100 percent in and behind what you are doing. How can you know this? Romans 8:14 gives the answer: *"For as many as are led by the Spirit of God, they are the sons of God."* Not only is it important that you know what God's plan is, but it is also of equal importance to know when, where, and with whom He wants it accomplished.

It all goes back to that intimate relationship with God. It's easy to get caught up in the busyness of life—even doing the work of the ministry—and run out ahead of God. The key is to abide in Him and stay in constant contact and communion with Him. He will lead you step by step so that the timing and all of the other factors are as they need to be for a successful outcome.

It is much like the military. The troops may be told about the overall mission, but they must wait for their commanding officer to tell them when to move, where to go, and how to accomplish their specific and individual assignments. A soldier doesn't just attend one briefing and then run off to accomplish the plan on his own. No, day by day he stays in contact with his commanding officer who coordinates the mission and leads him—and his fellow soldiers—to victory.

Whether you are an armorbearer serving the head of a ministry or you are teaching a Bible study through your local church, it is vital for you to stay in touch with headquarters. Only then can you know the master plan, stay on course, and achieve victory.

Developing the Spirit of an Armorbearer

The following are some words of wisdom for you to meditate on as you reevaluate your life and ministry:

- *"For we are not ignorant of his [satan's] devices"* (2 Corinthians 2:11).

- *"For if we would judge ourselves, we should not be judged"* (1 Corinthians 11:31).

- *"Search me, O God, and know my heart: try me, and know my thoughts: and see if there be any wicked way in me, and lead me in the way everlasting"* (Psalm 139:23-24).

- *"And when he putteth forth his own sheep, he goeth before them, and the sheep follow him: for they know his voice. And a stranger will they not follow, but will flee from him: for they know not the voice of strangers"* (John 10:4-5).

Dear God, in my mind, I know it is foolishness to get ahead of You, but walking that out every day is not so simple. Show me the things I can change so that I can spend more time communing with You. Help me become more sensitive to Your voice every day so that I readily recognize and obey it. If I start to go off on my own, I ask the Holy Spirit to give me a check in my spirit, and I commit to obey You. I don't want to build the ministry in vain. I want to be an extension of You building it so that You get all the glory. Amen.

THE HOUR OF THE LOCAL CHURCH

As each of you has received a gift (a particular spiritual talent, a gracious divine endowment), employ it for one another as [befits] good trustees of God's many-sided grace—faithful stewards of the extremely diverse [powers and gifts granted to Christians by] unmerited favor (1 Peter 4:10 AMP).

From the prophetic signs happening every day, it seems Jesus is soon to return. That is why I feel such an urgency about each member of the Body of Christ finding his place and remaining faithful, so we can be productive in God's Kingdom. I believe this is the hour of the local church.

The local church is the *hub* from which all ministry gifts are to function and the center out of which they are to flow. In the local church, you find what is needed to build the character of Christ in us.

Each member of the Body of Christ should discover his gift and calling and become fully connected to a local church. These members are then to submit one to another and to the God-called pastors and leaders there.

When I was serving as associate pastor and people would come into my office desiring to become part of our local church body, my first question was, "What church do you come from, and who was your pastor?"

You can tell what type of Christian you are dealing with by the answer you get. Millions of Christians attend church services only on Sunday mornings and are not committed physically or spiritually to that church. Their reasons for attending range from tradition to religious duty to social acceptance in the community. Going to church once a week eases their consciences of religious obligations.

Think what could happen in this country if those people would get on fire for God and begin to release their gifts and talents in the Body! We would see the world reached much more quickly with the Gospel.

Developing the Spirit of an Armorbearer

You may feel that you have nothing to offer your local church, but that is never true of anyone. Each born-again believer has something to offer that is unique. Each Christian has a call on his life, which will become apparent once he is involved in a church. Ask yourself these questions:

- What part am I to play?

- Where can I get involved?

- What resources do I have available?

- What opportunities lie before me?

- What do the leaders of my local church need from me?

- How many times have they asked me for help? How many times have I volunteered?

The key is to start where you are. The best way to step into the ministry God has for you is to ask leadership where you can help.

Father God, thank You that according to First Peter 4:10, I have already received "a particular spiritual talent," which can be employed to bless others within my local church. Lead me to the right leader under whom You'd have me serve, and guide me to opportunities to exercise this gift. I offer it freely to bless others and to glorify You. Amen.

ARMORBEARERS ARE VITAL FOR CHURCHES

Whatever your hand finds to do, do it with all your might (Ecclesiastes 9:10 NIV).

You have a talent that your pastor and your local church need to help reach your city. Each church has a vision that is given to the pastor by the Holy Spirit, and the pastor should take the time to share that vision with his church. Then members of the congregation should seek the Lord Jesus Christ to discover where they fit into that vision.

Opportunities to get involved are unlimited. Most local churches have departments, activities, or outreach ministries into which church members can fit. Here are some of the departments often found in a local church:

Benevolence (food/clothing)
Bookstore
Children's ministry
Christian school

Counseling
Discipleship
Evangelism ministry
Financial counseling
Greeters
Hospital/Shut-in visitation
Housekeeping
Intercession
Ladies Bible study
Maintenance
Marriage builders
Ministry to members of the military
Music ministry (such as choir or orchestra)
Prison/jail ministry
Publications
School of world evangelism
Security
Seniors
Singles 1 (20–24)
Singles 2 (25–39)
Singles 3 (40–50)
Sound ministry
Tape/CD duplication
Television
Temporarily impaired
Ushers
Visitor center
Youth

Churches may offer more or fewer avenues of Christian work, but there are always opportunities available that require people who are willing to release their talents. Without those who get involved, the church cannot function and the Gospel will not be preached to our cities. Pastors and leaders in the majority of churches have been bearing the brunt of the work of the ministry. That is why you hear of so many ministers "burning out."

Pastors and other spiritual leaders should be *breaking through,* not burning out. Spiritual and natural breakthroughs will happen as the Body of Christ decides to do its full part. Are you doing yours?

Developing the Spirit of an Armorbearer

- Do you sense a stirring to get involved in one of the areas of ministry listed above? Is there an area of need that this list doesn't cover?

- Ask yourself some questions:

  * Into what area(s) would my gifts fit best?

  * In what way will my involvement lighten the pastor's load?

  * Am I willing to be committed over a long period of time? Or does a short-term commitment fit my present situation in life?

* Whom else do I know who might be interested in getting involved?

Heavenly Father, thank You for the good plans You have for me. Help me to recognize my gifts and talents, and show me where I can put them to good use in my local church. Show me what I can do to assist my pastor and lighten his load. I want to contribute to his break-through and help him avoid burnout. Help me develop my gifts to their fullest potential so that the most people can be reached with the Gospel. Amen.

SUCCESSFUL KEYS TO LONGEVITY

AN OVERVIEW, PART 1

*Many a man claims to have unfailing love, but a faith-
ful man who can find* (Proverbs 20:6 NIV).

I went to Agape Church in Little Rock two weeks after it
was started in May of 1979. As soon as I arrived, I began
to get involved. I set out to do whatever I could do to help
my pastor fulfill his vision for the church.

In all I served 23 years in that ministry, and I saw God
faithfully fulfill His call on my life. In short, I bloomed
where God had planted me.

While preparing to speak to our office and ministerial
staff one day, the Holy Spirit put it into my heart to ask them
each to give me two keys that had produced longevity in
their positions and had helped them bloom where they were
planted. There were several full-time staff members who had
been with the church for many years. The church staff overall had remained—and still is—very solidly committed.

From that meeting came 40 keys to producing longevity
of service in the place where God has placed you. Here are

the first 20 of those keys in the order in which they were given.

1. You must have a call from God.

2. Make sure you have a real, personal relationship with Christ.

3. Ask God to give you His vision or goal for your life.

4. Be willing to do whatever is asked.

5. Do not lose sight of the people behind the work.

6. Be thankful for your position and never take it for granted.

7. Be willing to submit to authority.

8. Know that you are in God's will.

9. Know that your rewards are laid up in Heaven.

10. Develop a servant's heart.

11. Walk without offense.

12. Serve as if you were serving Jesus Himself, and do not get your eyes on the man under whom you work. On the other hand, be careful to respect the call that is on his life.

13. Be patient.

14. Have a loyalty that goes beyond personal feelings.

15. Respect everyone.

16. Hear no evil, see no evil, and speak no evil.

17. Judge yourself.

18. Do not ever be too big to do the small things or too small to do the big things.

19. Commit to the ministry the way a person should be committed to his marriage.

20. Know that you are important and needed.

Developing the Spirit of an Armorbearer

- Consider each of the keys above and evaluate how well you are doing at developing longevity and faithfulness in service.

- Read and meditate on what the Bible says about the faithful:

"A talebearer revealeth secrets: but he that is of a faithful spirit concealeth the matter" (Proverbs 11:13).

"A wicked messenger falleth into mischief: but a faithful ambassador is health" (Proverbs 13:17).

"A faithful witness will not lie: but a false witness will utter lies" (Proverbs 14:5).

"As the cold of snow in the time of harvest, so is a faithful messenger to them that send him: for he refresheth the soul of his masters" (Proverbs 25:13).

"Moreover it is required in stewards, that a man be found faithful" (1 Corinthians 4:2).

"And I thank Christ Jesus our Lord, who hath enabled me, for that he counted me faithful, putting me into the ministry" (1 Timothy 1:12).

Heavenly Father, You are such a faithful God, and I know it blesses You when we follow Your example and are faithful like You. I am committed to being an excellent armorbearer for the long haul. Show me if there are any blind spots so that I can deal with whatever would hold me back from serving You 100 percent. Amen.

AN OVERVIEW, PART 2

A faithful man will be richly blessed (Proverbs 28:20 NIV).

God is calling for many Christians to become armor-bearers for their leaders and for each other. We should begin to work as a team to advance God's Kingdom in the earth. The following are the remaining 20 of 40 keys that the staff of Agape Church believed enabled them to produce longevity in ministry:

1. Help other people fulfill their ministries.

2. Do everything you know to do to get where you want to be.

3. Do your very best wherever you are.

4. Stay with something until the job is finished.

5. Never quit.

6. Be dependable.

7. Be a good follower as well as a good leader.

8. Maintain your joy in the Lord.

9. Always remain sensitive to the Holy Spirit.

10. Always obey God's specific instructions.

11. Be patient with one another.

12. Always walk in love.

13. Be willing to change direction.

14. Know that God is your Source.

15. Use all the abilities that God has given you.

16. Have a healthy perspective of yourself.

17. Always keep the overall vision of the church before you.

18. Maintain a good attitude.

19. Trust in God's grace and His anointing on your life.

20. Be big enough to be rebuked and corrected.

Developing the Spirit of an Armorbearer

- Consider each of the keys above and evaluate how well you are doing at developing longevity and faithfulness in service.

- Read and meditate on the rewards for the faithful:

"O love the Lord, all ye his saints: for the Lord preserveth the faithful, and plentifully rewardeth the proud doer" (Psalm 31:23).

"Mine eyes shall be upon the faithful of the land, that they may dwell with me: he that walketh in a perfect way, he shall serve me" (Psalm 101:6).

"Anyone who refuses to slander others, does not listen to gossip, never harms his neighbor, speaks out against sin, criticizes those committing it, commends the faithful followers of the Lord, keeps a promise even if it ruins him, does not crush his debtors with high interest rates, and refuses to testify against the innocent despite the bribes offered him—such a man shall stand firm forever" (Psalm 115:3-5 TLB).

"For if we are faithful to the end, trusting God just as we did when we first became Christians, we will share in all that belongs to Christ" (Hebrews 3:14 TLB).

Heavenly Father, when You think of me, I want You to think of me as one of Your good and faithful servants. I want to lighten the load of the one You've called me to support and be someone he knows he can rely on over the long haul. Help me to develop all of the keys to longevity so that my life is truly a blessing to my leader and others. Amen.

GOD'S SEEDS

He answered and said unto them, He that soweth the good seed is the Son of man; the field is the world; the good seed are the children of the kingdom; but the tares are the children of the wicked one (Matthew 13:37-38).

Y

You can see that in God's hands we are "seed," and the world is His field. He wants us to put our lives in His hands and let Him plant us into the world. God determined the type of seed you are and where you are to be planted.

Genesis 1:11 says that the *"seed is in itself."* A seed of corn is always going to produce only corn, a kernel of wheat will produce wheat, and a grain of rice will produce rice. You cannot get rice from corn. So it is in the mind of God. He planned our lives before the world was created. Now He wants to plant each of us, so we can begin to bloom and bring forth fruit in season.

If you take a quick look at how a seed produces, it will give you some spiritual insight. The first thing that happens when a seed is planted into the ground is that it goes through a process of dying. Then, a rootlet will begin to push its way through the earth as the rain and sunshine give life to it.

Does that seed ever think, *Am I going to get through all of this dirt on top of me? It is so hard, and I feel hopeless.* Of course not. But then one day it happens. The seed comes forth, and the bud breaks into the sunlight. Many members of the Body of Christ are like that seed—all they see is dirt piled on top of them. Even staff members of ministries sometimes feel mistreated and left out. Perhaps they feel God has forsaken them because all they can see is dirt. Does this describe you?

If you will just stay where God has planted you and be faithful during the hard times, you will come forth. A seed is destined to spring forth if it is planted into good soil. If you know you are in the will of God and are where He wants you to be, then you *will* come forth, because it is God's destiny at work in you.

Developing the Spirit of an Armorbearer

- Where would you say you are in the seedtime and harvest process?

- Be encouraged by God's Word: *"And he said, So is the kingdom of God, as if a man should cast seed into the ground; and should sleep, and rise night and day, and the seed should spring and grow up, he knoweth not how.*

For the earth bringeth forth fruit of herself; first the blade, then the ear, after that the full corn in the ear. But when the fruit is brought forth, immediately he putteth in the sickle, because the harvest is come" (Mark 4:26-29).

- For a plant to grow healthy and strong, it needs plenty of water and sunshine. Drink in both today through meditating on these verses:

"For I will pour water upon him that is thirsty, and floods upon the dry ground: I will pour my spirit upon thy seed, and my blessing upon thine offspring: and they shall spring up as among the grass, as willows by the water courses" (Isaiah 44:3-4).

"For the Lord God is a sun and shield: the Lord will give grace and glory: no good thing will he withhold from them that walk uprightly" (Psalm 84:11).

Father, it isn't always easy to bloom where You've planted me. Sometimes I feel like I am two feet underground in the dark, surrounded by dirt. Like a seed has to die, I often have to die to my flesh and my own desires to fulfill my assignment to my leader. But I am encouraged that You are shining upon me and pouring out the water of Your Word upon me that I may bloom in due season. Amen.

BE LIKE A TREE

And he shall be like a tree planted by the rivers of water,
that bringeth forth his fruit in his season; his leaf also
shall not wither; and whatsoever he doeth shall prosper
(Psalm 1:3).

God wants His children to grow up and be like trees planted by rivers of water. Have you ever noticed that a tree *never moves?* We have beautiful trees in our yard, but I have never driven home and found that one of those trees had moved to my neighbor's yard because it did not like where it was planted.

Yet, in the Body of Christ—and even on church staffs—the first time someone is offended, he pulls up his roots and moves somewhere else. Then he wonders why there is no fruit in his life.

If a tree is continually uprooted and replanted, eventually the roots will die. Sadly, many Christians have experienced this. Because things don't go exactly like they think they should, they constantly jump from one church to another. They refuse to submit to authority, or they feel they have special gifts for the church that the pastor is not willing to recognize.

That kind of attitude keeps a person from fulfilling the divine, Heaven-ordained call that God has placed on his life. We must judge ourselves and be willing to die to our own purposes and dreams to let God's will be done, no matter the personal cost.

Make that commitment today, then dig deep.

Developing the Spirit of an Armorbearer

Can you relate to the tree that is constantly being uprooted, or are you allowing your roots to go deep and strong where God has planted you? Let the following verses encourage you to remain steadfast:

- *"And I pray that Christ will be more and more at home in your hearts, living within you as you trust in him. May your roots go down deep into the soil of God's marvelous love"* (Ephesians 3:17 TLB).

- *"A man shall not be established by wickedness: but the root of the righteous shall not be moved"* (Proverbs 12:3).

- *"Behold, a sower went forth to sow; and when he sowed, some seeds fell…upon stony places, where they had not much earth: and forthwith they sprung up, because they*

had no deepness of earth: and when the sun was up, they were scorched; and because they had no root, they withered away" (Matthew 13:3-6).

- *"The wicked desireth the net of evil men: but the root of the righteous yieldeth fruit"* (Proverbs 12:12).

Heavenly Father, let it never be said of me that my walk with You is shallow with no lasting fruit. As I am faithful to follow You and to remain steadfast in the place You've called me to be, may my roots go deep into the soil of Your Kingdom. I want to grow strong, stately, and steadfast as a tree planted by the water. I pray that I will bear abundant fruit that will feed many and that I may provide shade and shelter as well. Amen.

IF YOU ARE SAVED, YOU ARE CALLED

Who hath saved us, and called us with an holy calling, not according to our works, but according to his own purpose and grace, which was given us in Christ Jesus before the world began (2 Timothy 1:9).

This, to me, is one of the most important Scriptures in the Bible as far as understanding your calling. God has saved you and called you. That means, if you are born again, you are called. You cannot stand before Jesus one day and say, "I was never called." He saved you and called you, according to His own purpose and grace.

You are not here by accident. You have a destiny in God to fulfill, and you must find out your purpose by seeking God. Then, you become the deciding factor in fulfilling that purpose.

It was the God-ordained, God-destined time for the children of Israel to go into the Promised Land when God took them there from Egypt. However, because of doubt and unbelief, they missed their purpose in life.

For 40 years, the Israelites walked in circles in the wilderness until all of the males older than 20 had died. People with no purpose tend to walk in circles, blaming their failures on God or someone else. They walk until they dig holes for themselves. Then, many times, they die full of bitterness, mad at other people and God.

Joshua and Caleb, the only two men of that generation who lived to see the Promised Land, were of a different spirit. They knew they had a purpose and a call on their lives and that by faith in God they could possess the land.

It is sad that Joshua and Caleb had to wait 40 years to take what rightfully belonged to them. They could have been enjoying their destiny, but they had to wait because of the whining and complaining of others.

Our text verse says that God's purpose and grace were given to us in Christ before the world ever began. God knew who you were before you were born. Before He ever said, "Light be," He knew you in His omnipotent mind. Never doubt that He has a purpose for you. You were born into this generation at this particular time for a reason. Once you know that reason, follow the example of Joshua and Caleb and go forth to possess the land God has for you.

Developing the Spirit of an Armorbearer

- Are there any things in your life that would hinder you from possessing your God-ordained destiny? If so, what are they?

- Are you willing to make any necessary changes so that you can possess the land God has for you?

- What can you do today as an act of faith in what God has called you to do?

- A good word to put into practice: *"Do all things without murmurings and disputings: that ye may be blameless and harmless, the sons of God, without rebuke, in the midst of a crooked and perverse nation, among whom ye shine as lights in the world"* (Philippians 2:14-15).

Father God, I am thankful that my life has purpose and that there is a Promised Land that You've destined for me. I am committed to being like Joshua and Caleb, strong in faith. I repent of grumbling and complaining and for any other thing that would cause me to spend years wandering in the wilderness. Instead, I choose to cooperate with Your Word so that I may dwell in the land that flows with milk and honey. Amen.

FOR SUCH A TIME AS THIS

From one man he made every nation of men, that they should inhabit the whole earth; and he determined the times set for them and the exact places where they should live (Acts 17:26 NIV).

They are questions basic to all of us and ones I asked God: *Why I am here? Why was I born into my particular family? Why am I here at this time?*

You see, you had nothing to do with it. God did not ask your opinion when He planned you and made you. It was all up to Him. Why were you not born in the days of Abraham, Moses, David, or even Jesus? Why were you not born in the fifteenth, sixteenth, or seventeenth century? Why did God put you in this last generation before Jesus returns?

I believe that when God created the world, He saw a time period in which sin would abound as never before, a time when great calamities would come upon the earth. He foresaw a time when the greatest deception would come to try the people of God, a time when gross darkness would overtake many and their love would wax cold (Matt. 24:12).

In the midst of seeing all this, *I believe God said to Himself, I am going to raise up a people who will not compromise My Word—a people with My Spirit, anointing, and joy to go forth in those days and usher in the greatest move of My Spirit that the world has ever seen. I will pour out My Spirit upon all flesh and raise up a glorious Church without spot or wrinkle* (see Eph. 5:27).

When God determined these things, He said it would be a "special" people to live in these days; and in His mind, He saw *you.* He saw you and put you into place for a divine purpose.

No matter what position you hold, you are there to produce for the Kingdom of God and bring the lost into the saving knowledge of Jesus. We must realize that we were called before we were born into our families, before we knew our spouses or anyone else who is in our lives. And we will, at the Judgment, give account to God for what we did with that purpose and calling.

Determine to live in such a way that when your time comes to give account, you can answer with confidence and know that you did all that God had for you to do.

Developing the Spirit of an Armorbearer

- What are your thoughts as you meditate on the text verse, Acts 17:26? When you think about your service to your leader in light of this verse, are there any changes that you need to make in your attitude or actions?

- When you really think about the fact that God placed you into your present family during this time in history, does it change the way you view your life? Does it affect how you see and relate to your family members?

- What contribution are you making into the lives of your leader, associates, friends, and family members? What is your God-appointed role in their lives? What blessing does He want to give them through you?

Father, I take my role in life seriously. I realize that there are certain things You want to do through me in the lives of my leader, associates, family, and loved ones. Reveal those things to me and show me how to accomplish them. You are the Potter, and I'm the clay. Perform Your Kingdom work through me. Amen.

ALL WILL GIVE AN ACCOUNT

For we must all appear before the judgment seat of Christ; that every one may receive the things done in his body, according to that he hath done, whether it be good or bad (2 Corinthians 5:10).

It is an awesome thing to think that I will stand before Jesus and give an account of what I did with the gifts God has given me and the calling on my life. My pastor will not be able to stand up for me and say that I was a good associate. My wife will not be able to testify that I was a good husband. Only I can answer the Lord.

He will say, "Terry, what did you do with what I gave you? Did you fulfill your assignment?"

For 23 years my assignment was to serve my pastor as the senior associate and executive director of Agape Missionary Alliance. The Lord told me to take the same vision, anointing, and integrity of that church and reproduce it in the world. In order to do that, my assignment today is to be the president of Focus on the Harvest Ministries and to conduct the Armorbearer Leadership Schools releasing the Body of Christ into the harvest.

To you who are reading this book, I say by the Spirit of God: As surely as you are reading this, you, too, will stand before Him and answer the same questions.

That is why our callings are so important and why we must endure hardships when they come. We must be determined to accomplish God's will in our lives no matter the cost. Hebrews 5:7 says, "Who in the days of his flesh, when he had offered up prayers and supplications with strong crying and tears unto him that was able to save him from death, and was heard in that he feared."

Jesus went through strong crying and tears to fulfill God's will. Yet many church and ministry staff personnel run from anything that is hard, saying that if it were the will of God, it would be easy! Well, welcome to the real world. It takes strong crying and tears sometimes to stay where God plants you and to refuse to move no matter the conditions. But the payoff will come when you stand before Him and hear those words every armorbearer longs to hear: "Well done, thou good and faithful servant."

Developing the Spirit of an Armorbearer

- If you were to stand before the judgment seat of Christ today, what would He say to you?

- Does it differ from what you want to hear Him say? Is so, what can you do in order to change that?

- Meditate on these verses to strengthen your resolve:

"Thou therefore, my son, be strong in the grace that is in Christ Jesus. Thou therefore endure hardness, as a good soldier of Jesus Christ" (2 Timothy 2:1,3).

"But watch thou in all things, endure afflictions, do the work of an evangelist, make full proof of thy ministry" (2 Timothy 4:5).

"As you know, we consider blessed those who have persevered. You have heard of Job's perseverance and have seen what the Lord finally brought about. The Lord is full of compassion and mercy" (James 5:11 NIV).

"We are troubled on every side, yet not distressed; we are perplexed, but not in despair; persecuted, but not forsaken; cast down, but not destroyed; always bearing about in the body the dying of the Lord Jesus, that the life also of Jesus might be made manifest in our body" (2 Corinthians 4:8-10).

Heavenly Father, when it comes right down to it, the only thing that really matters to me is to hear You say, "Well done, thou good and faithful servant," when I stand before the judgment seat of Christ. Help me to fulfill Your call on my life and to put the gifts You've given me to their best use. You always cause me to triumph in

Christ, so I will endure hardness as a good soldier of Jesus Christ for Your glory. Amen.

TEACH US TO PRAY

And it came to pass, that, as he was praying in a certain place, when he ceased, one of his disciples said unto him, Lord, teach us to pray (Luke 11:1).

If you are going to go the distance and build longevity into your life, your personal relationship with Christ must be a priority. It is easy to stay so involved with the work of the ministry that we overlook our intimate times with Jesus. The pace can become so hectic that our lives resemble a never-ending merry-go-round.

I find it very interesting that in Luke 11:1, the disciples asked Jesus to teach them how to pray. Jesus' ministry was very well known at that time, with miracles, signs, and wonders occurring regularly. However, the Bible never says even one time that the disciples asked Jesus for His *anointing*.

Today, we see great men of God flowing in major healing and deliverance anointings. It is amazing how many people I hear who desire, covet, want—and would do anything—if these ministers would lay hands on them and "transfer" the anointing.

No one alive has ever flowed in the gifts of the Holy Spirit to the degree that Jesus did. If we covet that kind of anointing, we must do as the disciples did and ask Jesus how to pray. We must follow the pattern set by Jesus. Ministers are falling because they have lost their intimacy with the Lord. Many have fallen into sin simply because they substituted the work of the ministry for an intimate relationship with Him. Don't allow yourself to fall into this trap!

We receive God's plan, will, and direction by establishing a habit of prayer and study of the Word. It is the way we become intimate with Him. Pressures are coming at Christians today in a greater intensity than we have ever experienced. That is because the devil knows his time is short. The key to our being able to walk in victory is to cry out, "Lord, teach us to pray," and then begin praying.

Take some time to do that right now.

Developing the Spirit of an Armorbearer

- A good way to learn how to pray is to study the examples of prayer in the Bible, such as Luke 11:1-4; John 17; Ephesians 1:15-19; Ephesians 3:14-19; Philippians 1:9-11; and Colossians 1:9-11. In addition, many of the psalms are prayers offered by David to God.

- Some also find it helpful to journal their prayers. This provides a written record of your thoughts as you pour out your heart to the Father. You can also record the things you believe God is saying to you. Through the ages, written letters have been the vehicle through which many intimate relationships have been nurtured. Why should it be any different between you and the Father?

Heavenly Father, like many other people, I want to flow in the anointing to set captives free. I will follow the examples of the disciples and develop my relationship with You through prayer and spending time in Your Word. I thank You that as I become more and more intimate with You, Your anointing will be a byproduct of our relationship as it was with the disciples. Amen.

A GOOD HABIT TO FOLLOW

Wait on the Lord: be of good courage, and he shall strengthen thine heart: wait, I say, on the Lord (Psalm 27:14).

You will have many opportunities to quit the position you hold. I have had times of trial and hardship when I prayed for God to let me leave. And I have found that the strength to stand, the strength to go on, and the strength to resist satan only come through prayer. In our quiet times with God, He gives peace and strength.

We must develop a heart that seeks after God. David, king of Israel, was known as a man whose heart followed after God. If we could interview him today, we might ask what his greatest goal was in life. Was it to be the greatest king? The greatest musician? The wealthiest man on earth?

David would answer with one of his psalms: *"One thing have I desired of the Lord, that will I seek after; that I may dwell in the house of the Lord all the days of my life, to behold the beauty of the Lord, and to inquire in his temple"* (Ps. 27:4).

237

David's quest in life was to have God's heart. If we are ever to be true successes in God's Kingdom, we also must know that our first ministry is to glorify and honor Him. First Peter 2:5 says that we are a holy priesthood and we are to offer up spiritual sacrifices, acceptable to God by Christ Jesus.

The first calling for all of us is to worship and honor the Lord on a daily basis. Jesus had a habit of spending time with Him. That was the key to His anointing, wisdom, and longevity as spoken of in Luke 22:39 AMP: *"And He came out and went,* [as was his habit] *to the Mount of Olives, and the disciples also followed Him."* Luke 21:37 further explains, *"And in the day time he was teaching in the temple; and at night he went out, and abode in the mount that is called the mount of Olives."* He was in the habit of separating Himself from the people to, no doubt, spend time with His Father.

Spend some time giving God glory and honoring Him today. Like David, seek after God with all of your heart and let it become a way of life.

Developing the Spirit of an Armorbearer

- We humans don't like to wait, but it is a good habit to get into spiritually. The adage "Good things come to those who wait" definitely applies. Set aside some time now to simply wait on God. Let Him strengthen you and renew your strength.

- Here are some verses about waiting on God that will encourage you:

"For evildoers shall be cut off: but those that wait upon the Lord, they shall inherit the earth" (Psalm 37:9).

"Lead me in thy truth, and teach me: for thou art the God of my salvation; on thee do I wait all the day" (Psalm 25:5).

"Wait on the Lord, and keep his way, and he shall exalt thee to inherit the land: when the wicked are cut off, thou shalt see it" (Psalm 37:34).

"But they that wait upon the Lord shall renew their strength; they shall mount up with wings as eagles; they shall run, and not be weary; and they shall walk, and not faint" (Isaiah 40:31).

God, waiting is not something that comes naturally to me, but it is plain in Your Word that waiting on You is a vital factor in living an abundant life. So I choose to wait on You now, to simply sit in Your presence and wait. Thank You that as a result, You will renew my strength so that I will not grow weary or faint. You will exalt me and cause me to inherit the earth. You will lead me into Your truth and teach me. Thank You for showing me how to make this investment in my life that will contribute to my longevity. Amen.

HAVE A VISION AND A GOAL

*Now there cried a certain woman of the wives of the
sons of the prophets unto Elisha, saying, Thy servant my
husband is dead; and thou knowest that thy servant did
fear the Lord: and the creditor is come to take unto him
my two sons to be bondmen. And Elisha said unto her,
What shall I do for thee? tell me, what hast thou in the
house? And she said, Thine handmaid hath not any
thing in the house, save a pot of oil. Then he said, Go,
borrow thee vessels abroad of all thy neighbors, even
empty vessels; borrow not a few* (2 Kings 4:1-3).

Having a vision and a goal is another important part of
developing longevity in ministry. The widow in this
passage was left with a choice: She could obtain a lot of vessels, or she could borrow just a few. She gathered vessels and
began to pour the oil. When did the oil stop? It stopped
when she ran out of jars. She held the key to her miracle.

She could have said, "It is too hot today to gather jars,"
or, "Elisha, I don't feel well," or, "I could only find one jar."

Whatever she brought in is what she received. If she had really known what God was about to do, she could have found a dry well and said, "That is my jar!"

Elisha would have laughed, and I believe God would have laughed as well. If you do not exercise faith in life to reach a goal or vision, you will never achieve it. You are going to have to get up and work toward your goal. God will bless what you do.

When I first went on staff at Agape Church, I did not know exactly what my goal and vision were. I knew that I had a desire for the mission field, but that was all. As I was becoming part of a new church, I could not expect to be sent immediately to the mission field. So I began getting involved by just locking and unlocking the church building and getting things ready before every service.

That was a small goal, but it was still a responsibility God gave me to do. I did that for three years, until He raised up a full-time person to take over those duties. In the meantime, doors to the mission field began to open to me. *You must start with what your hand finds to do* (see Eccles. 9:10).

If you will go to your pastor or church leaders and begin to serve them, the vision God has for you will begin to take shape and come to pass. Be a blessing in your local church, and you will find doors opening up in all directions. What you make happen for someone else, God will make happen for you.

Developing the Spirit of an Armorbearer

- Has God given you a vision and a goal for this season in your life? What are they?

- Are you currently doing what your hand has found to do? If so, are you doing it with all your might? What are some ways you can improve things even more?

- If you haven't found a place to plug in, make it a point to contact your pastor or other church or ministry leaders and ask how you can be of assistance.

- Are you experiencing a personal crisis as the woman was in the text? If so, what could be considered "jars" in your situation? Boldly believe that God will perform His Word for you. Don't gather just a few "jars." Gather as many as you can!

Dear God, I want to do everything I can with what You've given me. Open my eyes to see all the avenues where I can be a blessing. As I am faithful with what my hand finds to do, I thank You for causing Your plans for me to take shape and begin to grow. Thank You for helping me to develop this key to longevity in my service to You. Amen.

KNOW THAT YOU ARE IN
THE MINISTRY THAT GOD INTENDS

On one occasion, while he [Jesus] was eating with them, he gave them this command: "Do not leave Jerusalem, but wait" (Acts 1:4 NIV).

Knowing that you are in the ministry that God intends for you is yet another key to longevity. In the days to come, everyone in some way must be connected with a local body under the leadership of a God-called pastor. Many people move from one ministry to the next, based on what they think each has to offer them—never asking what God wants. Using ministries as stepping stones is wrong, and if you are not prospering in your call, this could be the reason why. This key applies to everyone, not just fulltime ministers.

When I graduated from Southwestern Assembly of God Bible College, I received a very good offer. The dean of the college told me that he wanted to recommend me to a very good church, and it would have been a great opportunity.

However, the only thing that I had real peace in my heart about was attending Rhema Bible Training Center in Broken Arrow, Oklahoma, near Tulsa.

I knew that if we moved to Tulsa, it would mean both my wife and I would have to find jobs. This move would be a real test of faith for us, especially when I had the opportunity to move immediately into fulltime ministry.

Friends would say, "Why are you going to a Bible school? You just graduated from college!"

But God had another plan. He was preparing my way to Little Rock via Tulsa. We must follow our hearts and not the offers. God holds the future, and the best future for you does not always hold what seems to be the best offer. The will of God is to stay planted where God has you until He says to move.

Developing the Spirit of an Armorbearer

- Do you "know that you know" that you are where God wants you to be? If so, rejoice that God has you there for a reason, one you may not fully understand yet. Be encouraged that He knows what He is doing. All you have to do is be faithful with the task at hand and stay put until He tells you to move.

- If you are not in the place you know you should be or if you are not sure, spend some time seeking God about it. It may require a step of faith, but obedience to be where God wants you is the path to the greatest blessing.

- Let these verses encourage you:

"For I know the thoughts that I think toward you, saith the Lord, thoughts of peace, and not of evil, to give you an expected end" (Jeremiah 29:11).

"And thine ears shall hear a word behind thee, saying, This is the way, walk ye in it, when ye turn to the right hand, and when ye turn to the left" (Isaiah 30:21).

"For as many as are led by the Spirit of God, they are the sons of God" (Romans 8:14).

"Follow the steps of the godly instead, and stay on the right path, for only good men enjoy life to the full" (Proverbs 2:20-21 TLB).

"O my son, be wise and stay in God's paths" (Proverbs 23:19 TLB).

Father God, sometimes I get impatient, but I choose to stay where You have me until You say it is time to go. Even when it doesn't make sense to my natural mind, the center of Your will is where I will stay because that is where the blessing is. Thank You for the Holy Spirit who leads me and guides me. He tells me when to stay and He tells me when to go, and I will obey. Amen.

TRUST IN GOD, NOT IN MAN

Cursed be the man that trusteth in man, and maketh flesh his arm....Blessed is the man that trusteth in the Lord, and whose hope the Lord is. For he shall be as a tree planted by the waters, and that spreadeth out her roots by the river, and shall not see when heat cometh, but her leaf shall be green; and shall not be careful in the year of drought, neither shall cease from yielding fruit (Jeremiah 17:5,7-8).

Making God your complete source is another key to developing longevity in your life as an armorbearer. Every Christian will be faced with situations in which he must decide to either trust God or put his trust in man. How God leads you to walk through your situation may or may not look like it did for us when Kim and I decided to move to Tulsa.

Although we were in the center of God's will for us, we were barely making it financially. There was even a two-week period where the only food we had was about eight dozen eggs. The bills were paid, but we had no money for food.

I wanted to cry to my parents for help, because I knew they would gladly help. However, I also knew that I would be trusting in my parents and not God. That's not to say that it would have been wrong to let my parents know what we were going through, but I knew God was teaching us a very important lesson in faith.

During this time a pastor telephoned me, offering me a nice salary to work for him. I told him I would go and visit with him about it, but when I hung up the phone, Kim said, "Terry, you know God wants us here. We can't even go down there and talk to that pastor about this."

After we prayed and made sure we were hearing from God, I called the pastor back and apologized for even offering to visit him about that job. I told him I knew God had called me to be in Tulsa. I never regretted that decision, because that is how God taught me to trust Him.

When we arrived in Little Rock and talked with the Caldwells about working for them, we knew it, too, would be a step of faith financially. But they knew and we knew by an inner peace that we were supposed to join them. We also knew that God would supply, and He did.

The bottom line is that God must be your ultimate source of supply and you must follow His leading in how you deal with situations. Only you and God know where the line is between trusting Him and trusting in man. But when you obey Him, your needs will be met and you will grow in faith.

Developing the Spirit of an Armorbearer

- Are you being tempted to trust in man rather than God? If so, how do you think God wants you to handle the situation?

- Are you willing to go with your heart and believe God, even though at times it seems impossible?

- Meditate on what God's Word has to say about Him being your source of supply in Philippians 4:19, Isaiah 1:19, and Second Corinthians 8:9.

Heavenly Father, You are my source of supply, and because of that, I am confident that You will provide for all of my needs according to Your riches in glory by Christ Jesus. I am not bound by or limited to the world's system, and I choose to trust You and not look to man. As long as I obey You, I can trust You to provide for me. You desire above all things that I prosper and be in health as my soul prospers, and for that, I give You praise. Amen.

GOD IS THE REWARDER

Therefore take no thought, saying, What shall we eat? or, What shall we drink? or, Wherewithal shall we be clothed? (For after all these things do the Gentiles seek:) for your heavenly Father knoweth that ye have need of all these things. But seek ye first the kingdom of God, and his righteousness; and all these things shall be added unto you (Matthew 6:31-33).

If you are to truly make God your complete source, you must have a revelation that though He may choose to use your pastor, your church, or your salary, they are not your source. On the one hand, if you put your trust in man, then man will be the limit of your supply. On the other hand, if God is your source, the supply is unlimited!

I have known people who volunteered to help in a local church, working for no pay, but doing it unto the Lord. Then, because of their faithfulness, they were given a paid position on staff. I'm not saying that every volunteer position will lead to a paid one, but with God as your source, if

He wants you to be part of the paid staff, you can trust Him for that promotion.

Unfortunately, I have seen some of these same people who were promoted to a paid position begin to think that the church owed them something. When they were expected to be on time and to put in a full day's work, they began to feel that the demands were too great and that they were worth more than they were being paid. They forgot that God was their source and that they were working for Him.

Do not allow anger to rise up in you against your leader when you find yourself in a situation where you must believe God financially. If you agreed to work for the salary offered by that ministry, you have no right to get angry when you face a situation of lack. You may certainly discuss the matter with your leader, but ultimately you must take your eyes off of him and put them on God as your ultimate source of supply.

It delights your Father when you prosper, and because a laborer is worthy of his hire, He will see to it that your needs are met and that you have plenty (Luke 10:7). Don't limit God. He can use a variety of avenues to reward and bless you. And He will, when you put your trust in Him.

Developing the Spirit of an Armorbearer

- Examine your heart and ask yourself some questions:

- Are you living more on the world's system of finance or on God's? Are you willing to stay faithful, even in the face of financial challenges? Do you really believe that God is an abundant rewarder?

- Meditate on what God's Word has to say about Him being your source of supply:

"And God is able to make all grace (every favor and earthly blessing) come to you in abundance, so that you may always and under all circumstances and whatever the need be self-sufficient [possessing enough to require no aid or support and furnished in abundance for every good work and charitable donation]*"* (2 Corinthians 9:8 AMP).

"For the Lord God is a sun and shield: the Lord will give grace and glory: no good thing will he withhold from them that walk uprightly" (Psalm 84:11).

"Some trust in chariots and some in horses, but we trust in the name of the Lord our God" (Psalm 20:7).

Heavenly Father, thank You for being such a generous and giving God. I am committed to being a faithful worker whether I am in a paid position or not. You are the One I work for, and You are the One who will see to it that I receive the appropriate reward. I will not worry about what I will eat or drink or wear or drive or where I shall live. Since You take such wonderful care

of each little sparrow, I know You will take care of me. Amen.

TRUST AND OBEY

But by the grace of God I am what I am: and his grace which was bestowed upon me was not in vain; but I labored more abundantly than they all: yet not I, but the grace of God which was with me (1 Corinthians 15:10).

Two more keys for developing longevity in your life as an armorbearer are to trust in God's grace on your life and always obey His original instructions. You have a grace on your life to do what God has called you to do, although you may not understand or realize it now. When I first went to work at Agape Church and sat down with my pastor, he asked me what my talents were. I was embarrassed because as far as I knew, I had little talent.

I said, "The only thing I can tell you is that I will be faithful, dependable, and never late."

He said, "That is what I am looking for."

At that point, I began to see the grace of God at work. When He takes your life, anoints you, and makes you into something you never thought you could be, that is His grace in operation.

When I wrote *God's Armorbearer*,[1] I was concerned that no one would read it. I wondered why God had even asked me to write it, because I do not claim to be a writer. That was in 1990, and to date, over 750,000 of *God's Armorbearer* Books 1 & 2 have been sold worldwide in 12 languages.

You also have talents in your life that will come forth as you trust God's grace in the small things. We are what we are by His grace. If you always obey His original instructions, you will see things begin to work.

Many times, because of an overzealousness to do great things for God, some start getting off the course He has set for them. The problem occurs when they wake up one day and find out it was not God's dream, but their own, usually resulting in a lot of wasted time and money. If this is the case with you, you must go back to what God spoke to your heart in the beginning. That is where you will find the peace of God and His prosperity.

Many believers say, "I feel led to do this" and "I feel led to do that." They move from one thing to another always "feeling led," but never by the Holy Spirit. If the Lord has told you to join a church and commit yourself there, then do exactly what He said. From there, God will direct you one step at a time and you will not miss Him. The key is to learn to walk in the Spirit and stay on course with what God originally told you to do.

Developing the Spirit of an Armorbearer

- What grace is on your life?

- When I first went to work for my pastor, I wasn't yet aware of my talents, but I committed to be faithful, dependable, and never late. Even if you are just starting off and are unaware of the grace that God has placed on your life, what kind of commitment are you willing to make?

- What did God originally tell you to do? Have you been doing that, or have you gotten off track?

- Meditate on Romans 1:5-6 and Romans 12:6-8 and how they apply to you.

Heavenly Father, You are the giver of all good gifts, and I thank You for endowing me with the grace, gifts, and talents I need to accomplish Your will in my life. I thank You that as I am faithful and committed to the plan You have given me, these endowments will become more and more apparent and bless many. Because I am Your child, I am led by the Holy Spirit. I will stay on the path You've revealed to me and not get off course. Amen.

Endnote

1. Tulsa, OK: Harrison House, Inc., 1990.

PATIENCE

Having then gifts differing according to the grace that is given to us, whether prophecy, let us prophesy according to the proportion of faith; or ministry, let us wait on our ministering (Romans 12:6-7).

Notice the last phrase of our text: "Let us wait on our ministering." Patience is another key to your developing longevity as an armorbearer. *Patience* means "bearing pains or trials calmly or without complaint; manifesting forbearance under provocation or strain; not hasty or impetuous; steadfast despite opposition, difficulty, or adversity; able or willing to bear."[1]

You can see where a lot of problems come from in our lives—we are not patient. Our flesh is not willing to endure hardships, and it is always looking for an opportunity to be personally exalted and promoted. But the Bible says to "wait on our ministering." God wants to develop His character in you first before He exalts your ministry. The hard part is that we want it the other way around—promotion first and character later.

As you determine to have the will of God operate in your life and you get connected to a local church, the opportunities to murmur, complain, and become impatient will be there. When these feelings come, we are often tempted to direct them toward those in authority over us. We feel that we have a call and a place in the church, but our leaders are not letting our gifts come forth.

Unfortunately, you may occasionally run into a leader who is a controlling type of person. But the bottom line even then is this: Did God call you there? If He did, it is probably for the purpose of learning patience.

If your leader becomes mentally abusive and gives himself over to that kind of spirit, God will work on your behalf. God is a just God.

Stay humble, fast, and pray to hear the voice of the Holy Spirit, and wait on God for your day of release. Keep hurt, bitterness, and unforgiveness out of your heart. It is difficult to make a right decision if you are emotionally distraught. Remember that God loves you and is on your side.

I have found that when I really want something to happen for me, when I really want a new door to open up, I first have to give it to the Lord. It is amazing, though, that when I do that, it is usually not long until the door begins to open. You must relax in God and in ministry and let His perfect timing take place. It is by faith and patience that you will receive the promise.

Developing the Spirit of an Armorbearer

- Does this devotion strike a chord with you? Are you feeling antsy and impatient? Are you tempted to grumble and complain? If so, go to the Father and discuss the situation with Him. Confirm that He really wants you where you are. Then make a decision to adjust your attitude to one that reflects the fruit of the Spirit.

- Give your desires for promotion and ministry to God, and trust Him to open the door for you at just the right time. Resist the temptation to run out ahead of God and open the door yourself.

- Be encouraged by what the Bible says:

"Humble yourselves therefore under the mighty hand of God, that he may exalt you in due time" (1 Peter 5:6).

"And whosoever shall exalt himself shall be abased; and he that shall humble himself shall be exalted" (Matthew 23:12).

"Better is the end of a thing than the beginning thereof: and the patient in spirit is better than the proud in spirit" (Ecclesiastes 7:8).

Dear God, help me to develop patience in my situation. You've shown me such wonderful things to come that it is often difficult for me to live in the now. I commit the dreams in my heart to You and allow You to help me

develop my character and the fruit of the Spirit. I will wait on You and rest in You, and I trust You to open the necessary doors at just the right time. Amen.

Endnote

1. Merriam-Webster Online Dictionary, s.v. "patience."

FLEXIBILITY

*Behold, I have set the land before you: go in and possess
the land which the Lord sware unto your fathers, Abraham, Isaac, and Jacob, to give unto them and to their
seed after them* (Deuteronomy 1:8).

Being flexible is another important factor in developing
longevity as an armorbearer. That means being willing
to change. Most people prefer to be secure, keeping their
own little worlds stable with little change. The problem is,
it is easy to get stuck in a rut and miss the prompting of the
Holy Spirit.

If you look back, you can see that God has moved in a
different way in each decade. In the 1960s, the Charismatic
Movement came about. The 1970s brought a revival of the
office of the teacher. The 1980s brought a new commitment
and a call to emphasize local churches. In the 1990s, the
Lord turned our attention to the harvest of the lost.

We can see how the Holy Spirit changes direction, and
you can see why we need to follow His leading to get into

position for the last-day harvest. If you are going to be in the move of God, you must find out where He is moving and follow Him.

You will face many opportunities to make a change, and those changes may come in a way that will require time for you to adjust. In order for us to grow, we must be open to search our hearts and let changes perfect us.

I believe God is challenging us to take steps of faith that we have never taken before. He wants to move us out of our comfort zone to enable us to reach more people. The children of Israel had it made as long as God provided a cloud over them during the day to protect them from the desert sun, a fire at night to warm them, and manna to feed them. But then God said it was time to change. He told them to possess the Promised Land, then took away their "securities" and told them that they were going to have to fight and take the land by faith.

What happened? They rebelled in unbelief. They had become too comfortable the way they were.

Your life and ministry will stop dead in its tracks if you do not accept change. If you are going to reach this generation, you will never do it with a mentality that is stuck in a previous decade. We must seek God for innovative strategies and be open to any necessary changes. It may not be easy, but God will give you the grace and enable you to move into your "Promised Land."

Developing the Spirit of an Armorbearer

- When you look back over your life, do you recall times of great change? Maybe you came to a fork in the road and had to make a choice. Maybe you were forced to make a change that you didn't want to make. How did you feel during those times?

- In looking back, describe the part God played in those changes. Can you see that His hand was upon you, even if you didn't know it at the time?

- Meditate on the following verses, keeping in mind the need to be flexible:

"Being confident of this very thing, that he which hath begun a good work in you will perform it until the day of Jesus Christ" (Philippians 1:6).

"I will instruct thee and teach thee in the way which thou shalt go: I will guide thee with mine eye" (Psalm 32:8).

"I prefer a flexible heart to an inflexible ritual" (Matthew 12:7 TM).

Heavenly Father, it is so easy to get stuck in a rut, but I know that Your ways are not stagnant. Help me recognize those times when You want me to make changes, and then give me the grace and strength to implement them. When You move, I want to move with You. When

267

You stay, I want to stay with You. Thank You for guiding me with Your eye. Amen.

KEYS TO
COMMITMENT

LOYALTY & FAITHFULNESS

A true friend is always loyal, and a brother is born to help in time of need (Proverbs 17:17 TLB).

The first key to commitment is a loyalty and faithfulness that go beyond *all* personal feelings. The dictionary defines *loyalty* as being "faithful in allegiance to one's government, faithful especially to a cause or ideal."[1] *Faithfulness* is defined as "allegiance to duty or a person, loyalty, complete trust."[2]

These definitions describe the heart of an armorbearer—someone willing to give of himself for others, someone who is dependable and loyal to his leaders and can be trusted with difficult assignments. The armorbearer's loyalty and faithfulness, of course, are first to God and then to man.

The prophet Daniel and the three Hebrew children refused to eat the rich food served to the king when they were held captive in Babylon. Much of the food was totally against the dietary laws given to Moses by God. I have wondered why the other young captives did not follow their example.

When you think about it, however, you can hardly blame them. Their country had been destroyed, their family members were probably all killed or least held captive too, and they were prisoners in a strange city. Perhaps they thought God had forsaken them and that there was no longer any reason to hold on to His laws. But Daniel remained faithful, and as a result, he was highly exalted in the midst of an ungodly nation.

Today, as an armorbearer for a church or ministry, when you are asked by a leader to do something, your attitude toward that person is a test of your loyalty to God. If you do not like something a superior asks you to do, you may think it is between you and him. But it is really between you and God, if you are where God has assigned you. Make changes in your attitude and in your obedience to God; then doing what you are asked to do will not bother you. Personal feelings must be laid aside when you make a decision to serve God in whatever ministry He puts you. After all, He knew the rules and regulations of that ministry before He put you there.

Faithfulness is something that has to be found, according to First Corinthians 4:2; and the Bible says that we are to know those who labor among us. (1 Thess. 5:12.) That is why your pastor and church leaders watch for faithfulness. When they find someone who has proven himself trustworthy in hard and difficult situations, they know that person is mature and can handle more responsibility. Then that armorbearer is a great blessing to them.

Developing the Spirit of an Armorbearer

• Take a look at four characteristics of a faithful man:

A faithful man knows how to keep his mouth shut (see Prov. 11:13).

A faithful man ministers strength to his pastor and church (see Prov. 13:17).

A faithful man always will speak the truth (see Prov. 14:5).

A faithful man is a humble man (see Prov. 20:6).

• A word to encourage you:

"He keeps his eye on all who live honestly, and pays special attention to his loyally committed ones" (Proverbs 2:8 TM).

Heavenly Father, Your Word says that a faithful man is hard to find, but I am determined to be one of Your loyal and faithful ones. I pray for the leader You've called me to serve, that You give him wisdom in all his ways. I submit myself to his leadership and obey his instructions as my service to You. Show me how to be a blessing to him. Amen.

Endnotes

1. *The Merriam-Webster Dictionary* 1998, s.v. "loyalty."

2. *The Merriam-Webster Dictionary*, 1998, s.v. "faithfulness."

DON'T BE TOO BIG OR TOO SMALL

Young men likewise exhort to be sober minded. In all things showing thyself a pattern of good works (Titus 2:6-7).

Another key to commitment is not to ever be too big to do the small things or too small to do the big things. This point came from the children's minister at Agape Church. When he came on staff, he was called to work with children. He was very content and happy with what he was doing, but one day he was asked to be on our children's TV program called *Kids Like You.*

Now this was all new to him. He thought, *There is no way I could ever be on TV and play a role as one of the main characters.*

But God was stretching and expanding him for the purpose of reaching more children. It is always in God's plan to exalt you, but you will find that you must expand. This man had never once thought about being on TV, but God had a plan. Sometimes we can miss God because when we see more responsibility, we are afraid we cannot handle it.

However, we cannot get to the place where we are too big to do the small things. Some leaders have the attitude that their position excuses them to do and say whatever they please. But the Bible is very clear that leaders have a judge also.

The law of sowing and reaping works for masters and servants alike (see Gal. 6:7). If you get lifted up by pride, you are destined to fall (see Prov. 16:18). If you are unteachable, you open the door to deception. Paul wrote that we should not think of ourselves more highly than we ought (Rom. 12:3). If we begin to think we are better than others, problems begin. Determine to keep a humble heart and think soberly about yourself; in time, God will exalt you.

Developing the Spirit of an Armorbearer

- Examine your heart. Do you tend to think more highly of yourself that you ought, or do you sell yourself short?

- Seeing yourself as God sees you—nothing more and nothing less—is a great step toward maturity, and it will go a long way in making you a valuable armorbearer. When God knows that He can trust you to have the proper view of yourself, He will be able to trust you with greater responsibility.

- Let these verses motivate you to walk in humility, and then claim the corresponding promises:

"A man's pride shall bring him low: but honor shall uphold the humble in spirit" (Proverbs 29:23).

"Whosoever therefore shall humble himself as this little child, the same is greatest in the kingdom of heaven" (Matthew 18:4).

"And whosoever shall exalt himself shall be abased; and he that shall humble himself shall be exalted" (Matthew 23:12).

"Wherefore he saith, God resisteth the proud, but giveth grace unto the humble" (James 4:6).

Heavenly Father, I know that in Your eyes, there are no big or little jobs. Obedience and the attitude of the heart are the primary things that matter to You. Help me to maintain a sober attitude toward myself so that I will always be humble enough to do the small things and never too fearful or intimidated to do the big things. I put my life into Your hands to do with me as You wish. Amen.

COMMIT TO THE MINISTRY
AS A PERSON SHOULD
COMMIT TO MARRIAGE

But what happens when we live God's way? He brings gifts into our lives, much the same way that fruit appears in an orchard....We develop a willingness to stick with things, a sense of compassion in the heart, and a conviction that a basic holiness permeates things and people. We find ourselves involved in loyal commitments, not needing to force our way in life, able to marshal and direct our energies wisely (Galatians 5:22-24 TM).

Another key to developing commitment as an armorbearer is to commit to the ministry as a person should commit to marriage. If you are married, of course, your marriage comes before your position in the Church; however, you should approach the work for the Lord with the same fervency.

Concerning commitment, I heard a story of a farmer with a chicken and a pig who loved him because he was so good to them.

On the farmer's birthday, the chicken went to the pig and said, "Let's do something special for him."

The pig replied, "That sounds great, but what can we do?"

The chicken said, "Let's serve him breakfast. I'll give him eggs, and you can give him bacon."

The pig said, "Wait a minute. You are only giving an offering, but you're asking me to make a total commitment!"

It will require a total commitment to be faithful and do what you are called to do. The strongest key to having a successful marriage is communication. Likewise, in working with your pastor and leaders, communication is a must. The reason for misunderstandings is a lack of communication. Jesus always took the time to communicate with His disciples. He knew that the continuation of His ministry depended on it.

This need for communication works both ways, of course. Workers need to let their leaders know of potential problems, and leaders must take the time to communicate what is in their hearts to their people. If a leader is truly joined to his flock as a shepherd, the sheep will know his voice. People cry for security. In the ministry, that comes from making a commitment to a leader and that leader making a commitment back to the people.

Developing the Spirit of an Armorbearer

- Is it difficult for you to make commitments and to follow through on them? If so, why?

- What has been your level of commitment to your job as an armorbearer? Are you as committed to it as a person should be to his marriage?

- If you have people serving under you, are you asking more of them than you are willing to give yourself?

- Are you faithful to communicate with your leader and those who serve under you? Do you need to improve in this area?

Dear God, I know that You take my position as an armorbearer seriously, and I take it seriously as well. I commit to being my leader's armorbearer with the same intensity that a spouse should commit to his marriage, although I am careful to give my marriage priority over my ministerial duties. Help me to be an effective communicator, and give me the wisdom to know what to say and when to say it. May my commitment comfort and strengthen my leader. Amen.

THREE FINAL KEYS

Servants, do what you're told by your earthly masters. And don't just do the minimum that will get you by. Do your best. Work from the heart for your real Master, for God, confident that you'll get paid in full when you come into your inheritance. Keep in mind always that the ultimate Master you're serving is Christ (Colossians 3:22-24 TM).

The final three keys to commitment are closely related. The first is to always do your best. It is a way that an armorbearer can show that he cares about the church as much as the pastor.

A visitor walked into our church one morning with a crying child. The woman seemed upset, so one of our nursery workers went out of her way to offer help to soothe the child so the mother could go into the service. There the woman made Jesus the Lord of her life. That nursery worker did her best to help. No doubt, she has a great reward waiting.

The final two keys are to stay with something until the job gets done and never quit or give up. Regardless of what the job is, when you are given something to do—just do it! Then, make sure you finish it. You will have many opportunities to quit, but a committed armorbearer never takes the easy way out.

When we began to build the present church building for Agape Church, the Lord said to construct it debt free, meaning much of the work depended on the voluntary efforts of staff and congregation. When we finally moved into the new building, it had no ceiling or carpet, which meant that the chairs had to be set up before every service and taken down afterwards, along with all of the sound and band equipment. Construction would resume the day after each service, covering the floor with dust that had to be swept before the next service.

When we began, we had plenty of volunteers, but as the months passed, the number of helpers dwindled. Regardless, it was my responsibility to make sure the job was done. It was a difficult season, but I would not trade it for anything. The "hardship" pulled things out of me that I did not know were there—some good, and some not so good. But through it, I learned that the only way to succeed is never to quit.

If you are truly committed to the leader God has assigned you to, you will always do your best, complete every job given to you, and never quit. You will have the privilege of dealing with pride, anger, bitterness, selfishness, and all the destructive things that are in human behavior. But once you learn to deal with these, overcome them, and let God work in you, then you will become more and more like Him.

Developing the Spirit of an Armorbearer

The following are some verses that will encourage you to do your best and never quit:

- *"Concentrate on doing your best for God, work you won't be ashamed of"* (2 Timothy 2:14 TM).

- *"Do your best, prepare for the worst—then trust God to bring victory"* (Proverbs 21:31 TM).

- *"To win the contest you must deny yourselves many things that would keep you from doing your best. An athlete goes to all this trouble just to win a blue ribbon or a silver cup, but we do it for a heavenly reward that never disappears"* (1 Corinthians 9:25 TM).

- *"Do you see what this means—all these pioneers who blazed the way, all these veterans cheering us on? It means we'd better get on with it. Strip down, start running—and never quit!"* (Hebrews 12:1 TM).

Heavenly Father, I am committed to do my best at all times, finish every job assigned to me, and never quit. That is easier said than done, but with You as the

285

strength of my life, I can and will do it. I am commit-
ted to being the kind of armorbearer that both You and
my leader can totally rely on. Amen.

KEYS TO ATTITUDE

WILLINGNESS TO DO
WHATEVER IS ASKED

If ye be willing and obedient, ye shall eat the good of the land (Isaiah 1:19).

An armorbearer's attitude is another key to his developing longevity. The first aspect of attitude is a willingness to do whatever is asked of you. This is what leaders look for in people who desire to get involved. This is an attitude we all must develop in our hearts when we work in the Kingdom of God. You may not think you have the talent or ability to do whatever is asked, but because you are an armorbearer, you will set yourself to do it *because* you are asked.

Not long after I went to Agape Church, I was asked to take care of the weekly bulletin. I have no artistic ability. The last time I had done anything with art was pasting valentines in the fifth grade! But I told my pastor I would be happy to do it. It took me a while, but I did it to the best of my ability because the church needed it to be done. Later, someone else came along with the necessary talent and took over that job.

By contrast, there was a time when I asked someone to help me with a particular job. The person replied, "I'm sorry, but that is not my 'grace' gift." That may have been so, but I was asking for help—not a word from God. However, that is the kind of attitude many people have, and that is why they are never used. What is on the inside of a person is more important than what is on the outside. The greatest blessing to me is when people want to know where they can help. Those are the people who end up in leadership positions.

The next time you are asked to do something by your leader, regardless of what it is, be willing to tackle it. If you don't know how to accomplish the task, there are plenty of resources to help you learn. The main thing is to have and maintain an attitude of willingness to do whatever is asked. That is the heart of a true armorbearer.

Developing the Spirit of an Armorbearer

- What is your first reaction when you are asked to do something by your leader or others? Do you automatically express a willingness to act, or are you consistently hesitant?

- If you are hesitant, what is at the root of your hesitation? Fear? Selfishness? Inferiority? Whatever it is, talk to God about it. Let Him help you develop an attitude that is eager to help where help is needed.

- Can it be said of you as it was said of these? *"But Paul said of the churches of Macedonia, For to their power, I bear record, yea, and beyond their power they were willing of themselves"* (2 Corinthians 8:3).

- *"Feed the flock of God; care for it willingly, not grudgingly; not for what you will get out of it but because you are eager to serve the Lord"* (1 Peter 5:2 TLB).

Dear God, I am eager to tackle any job asked of me. I may not know how to do a thing and I might even be intimidated or afraid, but You are my help. I can do all things through Christ who strengthens me. If I don't know how to accomplish what is asked of me, I pray that You will lead me to the information I need. When I step out in faith, I believe You will help complete the task in a manner that will bring You glory. Amen.

NEVER LOSE SIGHT OF THE
PEOPLE BEHIND THE WORK

But Martha was worrying over the big dinner she was preparing. She came to Jesus and said, "Lord, doesn't it seem unfair to you that my sister just sits here while I do all the work? Tell her to come and help me." But the Lord said to her, "My dear Martha, you are so upset over all these details! There is really only one thing worth being concerned about. Mary has discovered it—and I won't take it away from her" (Luke 10:40-42 NLT).

In developing an attitude that will contribute to the longevity of an armorbearer, it is important never to lose sight of the people behind the work. This thought came from one of our computer operators who sat day after day keying information for the ministry into the computer. She said the Lord had helped her not to just type in name after name, but to be concerned about these people and to pray for them. You must not let what you do in the church become just another job.

Church workers must get a revelation of the people involved. They must know that they are working for *people,* loving *people,* and daily giving their lives for *people,* all of whom God loves. Without people, there would be no churches. People are the reason we are called to work in the Kingdom.

For example, it takes a lot of work to get ready for the annual Campmeeting at Agape Church. For me, sometimes the best feeling about Campmeeting came when it was over! But, that was a wrong attitude, and it arose because I let myself get caught up in all of the work and responsibility. My focus was not on people.

I am sure there were times when the disciples felt the same way, perhaps after Jesus fed thousands of men with loaves and fishes, not counting the women and children. When those meals were over and the leftovers gathered up in baskets, I expect that the disciples were glad it was over. But just think, they had a part in a wonderful miracle.

That is what you must always think: *here is an opportunity to minister to more people, and God is letting me have a part.*

If you get upset at all of the work you have to do, then you need to judge your heart's attitude. It could be that you are losing sight that *people* are the reason *for* the work. Never forget: all of that work you do as an armorbearer is changing people's eternal destiny—a privilege that is definitely worth the effort.

Developing the Spirit of an Armorbearer

- Today, in the midst of your busyness, stop yourself and focus on the people around you, the people you work for, the people who benefit from what you do. Thank God for the opportunity to impact their lives.

- Make it a point to pray for each person you come into contact with. The prayers don't have to be lengthy ones, but taking a moment to focus on each person's needs will help you keep in perspective the reason you do what you do.

Heavenly Father, people are what make Your heart sing. They are the reason You do all that You do. Help me never to lose sight of that in my service as an armorbearer. It is so easy to get caught up in my to-do list, deadlines, and putting out fires; but the people are the primary thing. Help me to be a blessing to my leader, my coworkers, and the people I serve. Amen.

BE THANKFUL IN ALL THINGS

In every thing give thanks: for this is the will of God in Christ Jesus concerning you (1 Thessalonians 5:18).

Being thankful for your position and retaining your joy are essential attitudes to develop if you are to be an armorbearer over the long haul. We should always be thankful for the place where God has put us. You may want a change in your life and position, but that will only come when you learn to be thankful for where you are. Not only are we to be thankful in good times, but we are to be thankful during difficult times as well.

I learned a valuable lesson on being thankful when I visited a missionary couple living in northern Romania. The lifestyle there is like going back in time a hundred years in the United States. The couple had to do all of their cooking and baking by hand, and they had five children.

The reason they endured such a difficult lifestyle was to raise up a church and a Bible school. For the first four months after they arrived in Romania, they had no hot water, and when they finally got a hot water tank, it broke after working only a short time. Then it took several weeks to get it fixed.

Observing their manner of life and their amazing attitude, I asked, "How do you do it?"

They looked at me and spoke a revelation to my heart when they said, "We have learned to be thankful. If we have no hot water, then we thank God we have any water at all. We pray in the Spirit one hour a day, and then we thank God continually."

That is an attitude that will cause you to win in any situation. And it will enable you to be an effective armorbearer for many, many years. The victory begins in thanksgiving.

Developing the Spirit of an Armorbearer

- Practice developing an attitude of gratitude today. No matter what difficulties you encounter, find something to be thankful about and voice your thanks aloud to God.

- Make a list of the five things you are most thankful for.

- Make a list of some things that you have taken for granted, but you should be thankful for.

- The following are some verses to "prime the pump" to get thanksgiving flowing if you are in the midst of a battle:

"I will give thee thanks in the great congregation: I will praise thee among much people" (Psalm 35:18).

"It is a good thing to give thanks unto the Lord, and to sing praises unto thy name, O most High" (Psalm 92:1).

"Enter into his gates with thanksgiving, and into his courts with praise: be thankful unto him, and bless his name. For the Lord is good; his mercy is everlasting; and his truth endureth to all generations" (Psalm 100:4,5).

"But thanks be to God, which giveth us the victory through our Lord Jesus Christ" (1 Corinthians 15:57).

Heavenly Father, I have so much to be thankful for! Forgive me for those things I have taken for granted. Thank You for allowing me to live in a free country where I can serve and praise You openly. Thank You for the opportunity to serve as an armorbearer and to have a role in what You are doing in these end times. When I run into difficulties and life gets hard, help me to see those things I can be thankful for. I am so blessed because of Your amazing love. Thank You! Amen.

REJOICE!

By him therefore let us offer the sacrifice of praise to God continually, that is, the fruit of our lips giving thanks to his name (Hebrews 13:15).

Paul wrote in Philippians 1:15-19 about some people who were preaching from a wrong motivation, which was to add afflictions to Paul who was in prison at the time. Instead of getting offended and having a bad attitude, he rejoiced over the fact that at least Christ was being preached.

If you are dealing with problems in your ministry or work, rejoice. It will strengthen you, and that strength will minister to everyone around you. You will have to fight to keep it, but it is yours. Remember, joy is not determined by circumstances.

Paul learned that lesson years before when he and Silas had been beaten with "many stripes" and cast into prison and their feet were fastened in stocks. Instead of sinking into depression, the two of them prayed and sang praises to God, loud enough that the other prisoners heard them. The result? There was a great earthquake that shook the foundations of the prison, opening all of the doors and loosing everyone's bands (see Acts 16:23-26).

Take a close look at the faith they exercised. Their backs were bleeding, they had been put in stocks, and all this for doing God's will. What a golden opportunity to complain and murmur. Instead, they began to worship God.

I imagine the dialogue between Paul and Silas went something like this:

"Hey, Silas, how are you doing?"

"I'm in pain, but I'm going to make it," answered Silas.

Then Paul said, "Silas, let's do something that is probably the most ridiculous thing you have ever heard of to do at a time like this. Let's start praising God."

"Paul, I think you're on to something. It is the most ridiculous thing I have ever heard of. But what better way to show our faith. I'm with you."

I can imagine Jesus looking at the Father and saying, "Do You hear them praising Us, Father? I know they are in pain and are suffering for My cause, but listen to that faith!"

However the dialogue went, we know that God was so moved that He sent an earthquake, and *everyone's* bands were loosed. If you need doors to open, then begin to worship and praise God. From that kind of praise will come deliverance for you—and everyone around you.

Developing the Spirit of an Armorbearer

- Right now, whether you feel like it or not, lay this book aside and begin to praise God. Lift your hands and your voice and rejoice in Him. It may be hard to get started, but if you will stay with it, rivers of living water will begin to flow out of you and you will be strengthened and refreshed.

- The Bible is full of examples of people offering the sacrifice of praise. Notice that rejoicing is something we *choose* to do.

"I will bless the Lord at all times: his praise shall continually be in my mouth" (Psalm 34:1).

"Rejoice in the Lord alway: and again I say, Rejoice" (Philippians 4:4).

"Consider it a sheer gift, friends, when tests and challenges come at you from all sides. You know that under pressure, your faithlife is forced into the open and shows its true colors" (James 1:2-4 TM).

"Although the fig tree shall not blossom, neither shall fruit be in the vines; the labor of the olive shall fail, and the fields shall yield no meat; the flock shall be cut off from the fold, and there shall be no herd in the stalls: Yet I will rejoice in the Lord, I will joy in the God of my salvation" (Habukkuk 3:17-18).

Father God, no matter what my circumstances are, no matter how difficult or hopeless they seem, I know You are working everything out for my good. You are turning things around for me, because I am the apple of Your eye. As an act of my faith, I rejoice in You, the God of my salvation. I offer You the sacrifice of praise. Amen.

HAVE A SERVANT'S HEART,
AS IF SERVING JESUS

Jesus said to them, "The kings of the Gentiles lord it over them....But you are not to be like that. Instead, the greatest among you should be like the youngest, and the one who rules like the one who serves. For who is greater, the one who is at the table or the one who serves? Is it not the one who is at the table? But I am among you as one who serves" (Luke 22:25-27 NIV).

Having a servant's heart as if you are serving Jesus is another important attitude for you to develop as an armorbearer. Jesus told the disciples that in the Kingdom of God, the greatest are those who serve. He even described Himself as one who serves.

Look at the life of Elisha, who began his ministry by serving Elijah for a number of years. When King Jehosophat asked if there was a prophet to go to for advice from the Lord, Elisha was named. It is interesting to note that neither the miracles Elisha had done nor his powerful anointing were even mentioned. Instead, a servant described Elisha as *"the son of Shaphat, which poured water on the hands of Elijah"* (2 Kings 3:10-11). In other words, it was his role as servant to a great man that was his recommendation. Elisha was Elijah's armorbearer.

That phrase "who poured water over Elijah's hands" became real to me when I visited Mike Croslow, one of our missionaries in Uganda. He took me out in the bush to preach in a village where there was no running water or electricity. It was not the end of the world, but you felt the end was visible from that place!

We preached under a mango tree to hundreds of people and had a wonderful time. When it was time for lunch, we went into a small mud church and sat down at a table. I did not see any utensils, so I asked Mike if there were any.

He said, "No, brother, you get the honor of eating with your hands."

Then a young boy of about 14 carried in a pitcher of water and a bar of soap. Since I was the guest, he came to me first, handed me the soap, and began to pour water over my hands. Then he continued around the room to all of the other ministers who were there. After that, food was brought in and we prayed and ate. When we finished, the young man came back and poured water again to wash our hands.

After that experience, I understood better the culture of the Middle East in the days of Elijah and Elisha. Elisha kept the prophet's house and did the cooking and all of the other menial tasks. Elisha truly had a servant's heart.

As you learn to serve, the anointing of God will increase on your life to help others. David became king and had a great anointing, but first, he was willing to give his life to protect his father's sheep. He didn't complain about having to take care of some stinking sheep.

Because he passed the test by having the right attitude, he was able to pass the test of Goliath when it came. You, too, if you will lay down your life to serve, will increase in anointing and be ready to pass the tests that inevitably will come.

Developing the Spirit of an Armorbearer

- What is *your* flock, or area of responsibility? Watching a group of toddlers every Sunday? Directing a choir, youth group, or children's church? Housekeeping, door greeting, or ushering? Your area of responsibility is your proving ground. If you function well as a servant, you will be promoted.

- God's Word on the matter: *"Serve the Lord with gladness: come before his presence with singing"* (Ps. 100:2).

Heavenly Father, thank You for the privilege of being a servant to my leader and others. Like Jesus, David, and Paul, I will serve You and my leaders. I determine in

my heart to pour water on the hands of my leader, knowing that as Elisha served, he eventually received a double portion of Elijah's anointing. I fully serve expecting You to bless me with a fresh anointing. I will serve You with gladness—during the good times and during the challenging ones. Help me to develop the servant's heart to the fullest. Amen.

SUBMITTING TO GOD'S DELEGATED AUTHORITY

Let every soul be subject unto the higher powers. For there is no power but of God: the powers that be are ordained of God (Romans 13:1).

If Jesus asked you to clean the church bathrooms, how clean would they be? If He asked you to help in the nursery, how well would you handle the children?

When you volunteer and are asked to do something, it is important to remember that it is as if Jesus Himself asked you, because whatever you are doing is for Him. According to our text, obedience to higher authority—from world governments to church governments—is ordained by God.

In order to properly submit to authority, you must have a clear understanding that the authority rests in the office, not in the man who holds the office. For instance, a former president cannot just drive up to the White House and walk into the Oval Office. He must go through the proper security protocol like every other citizen because he is no longer in authority.

When God told Moses to speak to the rock in Numbers 20:8–29, both he and Aaron rebelled. Moses angrily struck the rock instead of speaking to it, and Aaron stood with him in this rebellion. As a result, God instructed Moses to take the high priest's robe off Aaron and place it on Eleazar. When that happened, Aaron died. This shows the seriousness of misrepresenting God before people. The authority on the high priest's office remained, but it was given to Eleazar.

The only time we are released from submitting to authority is if that authority violates the Word of God. Then we are not required to submit, because we have a *higher* authority. But, that is not usually the case. Rebellion usually starts when a person has a problem with the requirements of joining the church, for example. Then this attitude carries over to the established guidelines in other areas.

Another more subtle—but just as real—type of authority is when the leadership says, "That is the way we do it around here." It does not matter whether you agree with the way things are done, you must submit if you know God wants you to be a part of that church or ministry.

To put it bluntly, if you get mad and speak against the leaders, then it is a form of rebellion. In reality, you are coming against God since He is the One who puts leaders into their positions. If you have a problem with something, make the effort to talk with the leadership in an attitude of love and let them explain why they do things the way they do. This understanding may make it easier for you to go with the flow. But even if you don't understand, in the end, the armorbearer must submit to the policies and methods that the leadership puts into place.

Follow the God-ordained chain of command. Then all things will be done decently and in order, and you will be a tremendous asset to your leader.

Developing the Spirit of an Armorbearer

- What is your attitude toward submitting to authority? If you have problems with it, talk to God and get to the root of the reason why. If you've been taken advantage of or hurt by an authority figure, let God minister healing to you. There is a godly pattern for submission and authority, and God wants to help you experience it, so you can reach your full potential.

- A word of instruction from the Bible: *"I exhort therefore, that, first of all, supplications, prayers, intercessions, and giving of thanks, be made for all men; for kings, and for all that are in authority; that we may lead a quiet and peaceable life in all godliness and honesty"* (1 Timothy 2:1-2).

311

Dear God, I realize that all power and authority come from You, and because of that, I choose to submit to the authority figures over me. I will be faithful to pray for them so that we may lead quiet and peaceable lives. Help me to honor them and to walk in love toward them. Amen.

FIVE STRUCTURES
OF AUTHORITY, PART 1

Submit yourselves for the Lord's sake to every authority instituted among men (1 Peter 2:13 NIV).

God has put into place five structures of authority, which we all must submit to and that serve as a framework for our lives. We will look at three of these—the authority of God and His Word, the authority of national and local governments, and the authority within the church or ministry.

1. *God and His Word* (1 John 2:3-4)

We must keep God's Word in our hearts and fully submit to the laws laid down in it because we will be judged according to it.

2. *National and local government* (1 Pet. 2:13-14)

The apostle Peter wrote that Christians must submit to *every* ordinance of man for the Lord's sake. For example, if you work, you must pay taxes; otherwise, you may go to jail. You may not like this, but you have to do it because it is the law. If we rebel against paying those taxes, we are really rebelling against God and not man. However, if laws are passed forbidding us to preach, for example, then those national laws have rebelled against God and we must obey the higher authority of His Word.

3. *The church or ministry*

One day in 1980, I was reading my Bible when I heard the Spirit of God say, *Have a Pastor's Appreciation Day.* I had never heard of such a thing, but I told the rest of the staff, and we worked it out.

One Sunday morning, I walked to the pulpit and you could see that my pastor was wondering what in the world was going on. Then I announced it was Pastor's Appreciation Day, and we blessed him financially by receiving a special offering. Also, we had people come up and share what his ministry had meant to them.

But, someone came to me who felt we were lifting up a man and not exalting Jesus. I searched my heart and the Bible and found several interesting verses pertaining to this.

First Timothy 5:17-18 states, *"Let the elders that rule well be counted worthy of double honor, especially they who labor in the word and doctrine. For the Scripture saith, Thou shalt not muzzle the ox that treadeth out the corn. And, The laborer is worthy of his reward."* By this I realized we were on target.

Pastors and ministry leaders have authority and must give an account of that authority. They deserve appreciation. Hebrews 13:17 says, *"Obey them that have the rule over you, and submit yourselves: for they watch for your souls, as they that must give account."*

I want to challenge everyone who reads this book to get together with others to show your pastors or ministry leaders that you love them. Pray and ask the Lord what He would have you do, and then bless them with the best you can. Do this once a year to encourage them.

You will find that God will honor this, and the love of God will flow in your midst.

Developing the Spirit of an Armorbearer

- Take a few moments and evaluate your level of submission toward God's Word, your local and national leaders, and your pastor and church or ministry staff.

- Repent of any grumbling or "bucking the system" you have given place to, and commit to submitting to God's chain of command.

- If the church or ministry you serve does not already have an Appreciation Day or something similar, pray about how God would have you and others bless your leader. Then spearhead the effort.

Heavenly Father, the chain of command is something that You instituted for our protection, peace, and well-being. I willingly submit to the authority of Your Word, my national and local leaders, and my pastor and church/ministry leaders. When I submit to them, I am submitting to You, and that is where the blessing is. Amen.

FIVE STRUCTURES
OF AUTHORITY, PART 2

Submitting yourselves one to another in the fear of God
(Ephesians 5:21).

God has put into place five structures of authority, which
we all must submit to and that serve as a framework for
our lives. Here we will look at the last two—authority
within the family unit as well as at the workplace.

1. *The family*

God established an authority structure for families,
which Paul wrote about in Ephesians. In Ephesians 5:22, he
wrote, *"Wives, submit to your husbands as to the Lord."* He
went on to say that husbands are to love their wives as Christ
loves the Church, so there is a responsibility on the part of
both spouses.

Paul then instructed children in Ephesians 6:1: *"Children, obey your parents in the Lord, for this is right."* As long
as you are living under the roof of your parents, you must

submit to them. If you are over 40 years old and still living with your mom and dad, then you will have to submit to them in many areas of your life. My suggestion is to move out. Once you are not living in their house, you are no longer under their authority. However, remember that the Bible says you are always to honor them.

2. *Employers*

Peter wrote that servants should be subject to their masters and not only to those masters who are *"good and gentle"* (1 Pet. 2:18 NASB). That makes it very clear that we must submit on our jobs to whomever is in authority over us. If your boss is harsh or demanding, don't complain, but pray that God will work in his heart and cause him to become good and gentle. Then make sure you are on time and do a good job. Your employer will be ministered to by your diligence. If you do this, God will more than likely open a door for you to share Christ with him, if he is not already a believer.

The Roman centurion who told Jesus to just "speak the word" and his servant would be healed understood authority. He was a man in authority and under authority himself. Jesus said He had not found anyone in Israel with this kind of faith. Why was his faith so strong? Because he understood authority. He knew that demons and disease were subject to the authority of Jesus (see Matt. 8:9-10).

In conclusion, we will never graduate from being under authority—even when we get to Heaven. But those who learn how to flow in submission to it are the ones who will climb God's ladder of spiritual authority and do exploits for Him.

Developing the Spirit of an Armorbearer

- How well does authority and submission work in your home? You may need to sit down with your family to discuss the biblical model and explain any changes that are needed. Make it a family affair.

- How well do you submit to authority at your workplace? Do you submit joyfully, or do your insides churn even though outwardly you conform? Pray for your boss and then make the necessary changes in your attitude. Submit to your boss as unto the Lord.

Dear God, it is often difficult to submit within my family unit and also at work. Sometimes the demands are unreasonable, sometimes I disagree, but I know from Your Word that I am to submit out of obedience to You. If there is an abuse of power or I am asked to do something that is contrary to Your Word, help me to respectfully decline. As I am faithful to submit to those You've put over me, I trust that You will promote me to a place of authority in due season. Amen.

BE BIG ENOUGH TO BE
REBUKED & CORRECTED

For the commandment is a lamp; and the law is light; and reproofs of instruction are the way of life (Proverbs 6:23).

The last key to maintaining a good attitude is being big enough to be rebuked and corrected. We will be reproved and corrected in life because we are human and make mistakes. If you want to mature, you must be teachable.

Proverbs 9:8-9 says, *"Reprove not a scorner, lest he hate thee:* **rebuke** *a wise man, and he will love thee. Give* **instruction** *to a wise man, and he will be yet wiser:* **teach** *a just man, and he will increase in learning"* (emphasis added).

If you are one who is going to rebuke, then be wise enough to *instruct* and *teach* as well. I have seen people who felt called to "rebuke," but they didn't take the time to teach or instruct. That kind of rebuke amounts to criticism, which wounds and results in nothing but strife.

God never assigned anyone to break another person's spirit. If the correction is abusive, then take it before the Lord and pray for wisdom in how to handle it. If it continues, then sit down honestly and openly with your leader and share with him how this has hurt and offended you. God sees both of your hearts. Do whatever is necessary to keep your heart pure. On the one hand, we are always to rebuke with meekness and love and take the time to teach people what they have done wrong and how to do it correctly.

On the other hand, if you are the one being rebuked, do not get your feelings hurt. Be big enough to take it and go on without holding a grudge and being defensive. It is very clear from the Word of God that a wise man will listen to correction and judge himself (see Prov. 13:1). A fool despises any instruction.

I must admit that I have met some fools in my life. They would not take any correction. Their shortcomings and problems were always someone else's fault. They were always right. What do you do with people like that? You stay away from them. They will never fulfill God's will, because they will not admit mistakes.

We are told in the Bible to judge ourselves and make corrections when we need to change. If you refuse to judge yourself, you will face judgment on the sin you are in.

I believe it is very important today to have people around us to whom we are accountable, people who can speak into our lives. That is why the Bible says to submit to God-called leadership, so they can help us if we begin to miss it. We cannot afford to miss the will of God in our lives.

Stay humble before the Lord, and when you are corrected or rebuked, receive it and learn from it. Then you will grow into the place God intends for you to be. There is no growth without some pruning. God wants lasting fruit to come forth in your life (see John 15:16).

Developing the Spirit of an Armorbearer

- Evaluate how well you take rebuke and correction.

- Judge yourself to see if there is any sin in your life. If there is, repent, receive forgiveness, and make the necessary changes.

- The following are some verses for additional study:

"The way of a fool is right in his own eyes: but he that hearkeneth unto counsel is wise" (Proverbs 12:15).

"He that refuseth instruction despiseth his own soul: but he that heareth reproof getteth understanding" (Proverbs 15:32).

"Smite a scorner, and the simple will beware: and reprove one that hath understanding, and he will understand knowledge" (Proverbs 19:25).

Heavenly Father, no one likes correction, but only fools refuse it. I choose to submit to godly correction and rebuke. Help me to judge myself so that correction won't be necessary, but if I overlook something and require a rebuke, help me to receive it humbly and to make the changes needed. Amen.

KEYS TO
TEAMWORK

COACHES IN THE PRESS BOX

I will instruct thee and teach thee in the way which thou shalt go: I will guide thee with mine eye (Psalm 32:8).

Another invaluable characteristic to help armorbearers develop longevity is teamwork. I want to share an analogy that the Holy Spirit quickened to me between an NFL football team and the operation of the local church. We will start with the coaches in the press box. It is their responsibility to choose the best plays to call, which they can do because they see the overall field and the way the opposing team is set up. Their job is to watch for any weaknesses, then quickly call plays to take advantage of them.

This could be compared to the Father and the Son of God, who sit in the press box and call the plays in our lives. They know the devil's tactics as well as which plays will be most effective against them. Paul wrote that we should not let satan take advantage of us, *"for we are not ignorant of his devices"* (2 Cor. 2:11).

327

There are three heavens in the universe (see 2 Cor. 12:2). The first heaven is over the physical earth; the second is the realm where satan, demons, and angels dwell; and the third heaven is the "press box" where God's throne is. The Bible makes it clear that satan is the prince and power of the air. God looks down on the second heaven and sees clearly the strategies of the devil against the Church.

God then calls down to the Coach on the playing field—the Holy Spirit in our analogy—and communicates to Him what the devil is doing. With this information, our Coach can then let us know what plays to run.

The coaches in the press box record every play on video, so they can take a look at the last play while another play is being run on the field. That way they can analyze what the opposing team is setting up.

Our Father has the ability to see past, present, and future. He knows the right play to call every time. It is up to us to listen to our Coach on the playing field. Our Coaches in the press box are essential if we are to win the game!

Developing the Spirit of an Armorbearer

- No matter what you are going through, your heavenly Coaches are in the press box of Heaven and see it all. They see every hurt, every joy, and every dilemma, and they know which calls to make. They will lead you to victory.

- Your Coaches also see your leader and the ministry for which you work. You can trust that They will communicate Their will and plan.

- Meditate on these verses about what the Lord sees.

"Behold, the eye of the Lord is upon them that fear him, upon them that hope in his mercy" (Psalm 33:18).

"He ruleth by his power for ever; his eyes behold the nations: let not the rebellious exalt themselves" (Psalm 66:7).

"Thine eyes did see my substance, yet being unperfect; and in thy book all my members were written, which in continuance were fashioned, when as yet there was none of them" (Psalm 139:16).

"For the ways of man are before the eyes of the Lord, and he pondereth all his goings" (Proverbs 5:21).

"The eyes of the Lord are in every place, beholding the evil and the good" (Proverbs 15:3).

Father God, I'm so glad You see the big picture. Often we humans can't see the forest for the trees, but You see it all. I trust Your judgment to make the most effective calls, and I pray that my leader will hear them clearly so he can communicate them to the team. Then help us to execute the plays well so we can win. Amen.

THE COACH ON THE FIELD

Howbeit when he, the Spirit of truth, is come, he will guide you into all truth: for he shall not speak of himself; but whatsoever he shall hear, that shall he speak: and he will show you things to come (John 16:13).

Developing teamwork is vital in conducting Kingdom business. In our analogy of a football team, the coach on the field assists in calling the plays, but his most important job is to communicate those plays to the quarterback. This coach is there to encourage and strengthen the team's confidence. He never leaves the field until the game is over.

The Coach on the field for the Church, of course, is the Holy Spirit. He is the Head Coach on the playing field with us. He is always encouraging us when we get tired or hurt. He will be with us until the game is over.

When a player is discouraged with his performance, this coach begins to build up his confidence. He will tell that player that he is going to make it, that he can win the game. That is the Word of the Holy Spirit to us—we can make it, we can win, we are the Lord's very best, and nothing is impossible to us with God on our side.

The Holy Spirit will only speak or call the plays that He hears from the Father. But when He hears them, He communicates those directions to the quarterback—or pastor or ministry leader—who in turn communicates to us, his teammates.

Developing the Spirit of an Armorbearer

- Think of some examples of when you distinctly heard the voice of the Holy Spirit. How were you able to tell that it was His voice?

- Keep in mind, anything the Holy Spirit says will line up with God's Word. He cannot speak contrary to it.

- The Holy Spirit is not an it. He is part of the divine Person of the Godhead and is capable of being grieved like a person (Eph. 4:30).

- Be aware that the Holy Spirit is with you every single minute. Remember: He will *never* leave the playing field until the game is over.

- Below are some verses to study and meditate on. Be mindful of the Person of the Holy Spirit with you today.

"Nevertheless I tell you the truth; It is expedient for you that I go away: for if I go not away, the Comforter will

not come unto you; but if I depart, I will send him unto you" (John 16:7).

"And I will pray the Father, and he shall give you another Comforter, that he may abide with you for ever" (John 14:16).

"But the Comforter, which is the Holy Ghost, whom the Father will send in my name, he shall teach you all things, and bring all things to your remembrance, whatsoever I have said unto you" (John 14:26).

"And thine ears shall hear a word behind thee, saying, This is the way, walk ye in it, when ye turn to the right hand, and when ye turn to the left" (Isaiah 30:21).

Heavenly Father, thank You so much for sending the Holy Spirit to communicate Your love, encouragement, and instruction to me, my other "teammates," and the "quarterback" of our team. Every day, help us to recognize His voice and to distinguish it from all the other voices in the world. I pray that we will follow His voice and the voice of a stranger we will not follow—in our personal lives as well as in the ministry we serve. Amen.

THE QUARTERBACK

It is a true saying that if a man wants to be a pastor he has a good ambition (1 Timothy 3:1 TLB).

In our illustration of how a football team mirrors our lives, the quarterback is the head communicator on the playing field. He must effectively call the plays given to him by the coaches. He must run the offense. He depends fully on the coaches to spot the weaknesses in the other team's defense in order to win the game. No team can win without a good quarterback, so it is essential that he be healthy and strong in order to win.

This quarterback represents the pastor or leader of a ministry. He must call the play for the team. He must depend on the Holy Spirit to give orders, then he must follow those instructions. Running the right plays and gaining yards will come by being obedient to the Holy Spirit.

As any coach runs his team a little different from any other, so will the Holy Spirit run each local church or ministry in a different way. What works for one will not always work for another.

The Holy Spirit wants the ministry leader to hear the plays from Him. After the leader has received the play, he must effectively communicate it to the team in order for the play to work. Many plays have failed and penalties have resulted because the players did not know the play or on what count the ball was to be snapped.

Ministry leaders must also hand the ball off to the other "backs," so that their abilities and talents can be used in gaining yards for the team. Any quarterback understands the gifts and talents that are there to assist the team, and he utilizes them to their full potential.

In our analogy, the "football" is the vision, and it must be handed to the other staff ministers so that they can "gain yardage." If a leader hangs on to the vision because of insecurity, he will hinder the team. No quarterback can win the game by himself.

In fact, if a head coach sees a quarterback refusing to hand off or throw the football to another player, he will discipline him and take him out of the game if the quarterback does not make the adjustments. The most valuable person on the team is the quarterback, who controls the offense. But the quarterback knows his success depends fully on those around him.

Developing the Spirit of an Armorbearer

- Points to remember:

1. No quarterback can win the game by himself. The other players must do their jobs in order to gain yards. Quarterbacks have been frustrated, bruised, hurt, and even knocked out of the game due to a lineman who let his defensive man through the line. Each player must do his job in order for the team to win.

2. The quarterback cannot do the job of a tackle just as a tackle cannot do the job of a quarterback. Each is gifted in his place. All must carry the same vision, and that is to score and to win the game.

3. Every quarterback must take time for a huddle. In the huddle, he communicates the plays so that each person knows his assignment for that down.

4. Regarding the office of the "bishop" (or the leader of a ministry) Paul said, *"He must manage his own family well and see that his children obey him with proper respect. (If anyone does not know how to manage his own family, how can he take care of God's church?)"* (1 Tim. 3:4-5 NIV).

Father, I pray for my leader that he will hear the calls You would have him make. Give him insight into all of the players on our team, and help him recognize each of

their strengths. Help him to be secure in the "quarter-back" position and never to feel threatened by any of the other members of our team. Show us ways to communicate our love and faith in him, and may he sense our support. Amen.

HALFBACKS,
FULLBACKS, & ENDS

Now the body is not made up of one part but of many.
The eye cannot say to the hand, "I don't need you!" And
the head cannot say to the feet, "I don't need you!"
(1 Corinthians 12:14,21 NIV).

Halfbacks, fullbacks, and ends are the next positions in our teamwork analogy. They, along with the quarterback, must advance the ball—the ball representing the ministry leader's vision. The backs and the ends must be strong, quick, and creative in making the right moves. They must not be concerned about which back is making the most yards. If one is having a good game, then he should be the one the quarterback gives the ball to. The goal is to win the game, not to be concerned with who is scoring. These players, like the quarterback, will receive the majority of the recognition due to their special gifts and talents.

The first thing they must do is take the ball from the quarterback. At that point, it is up to them to think quickly and creatively in order to move the ball down the field. They depend on the linemen to clear the way for them, making it possible to score. Each team member must be mindful of the basics. To forget or ignore them can result in a fumble.

These halfbacks, fullbacks, and ends represent the associate ministers. They are gifted by God to run with the vision and effectively communicate it to the people. They have the freedom to think creatively but must remember to listen to the play that the leader calls. Then they can take the handoff.

No halfback or fullback will call the play; it is always the quarterback. The different backs have the right to give input to the quarterback or tell him that they are open and can break through the line, but it is still up to the quarterback to call the play.

If the associates take the handoff from the leader, then run in a direction opposite of the play, there will be major problems. They must go in the direction of the team. Just as a quarterback will be set down by the head coach if he does not listen to the play, so will the associates be set down by their leader and the Holy Spirit if they try to do their own thing.

The football itself represents the vision of the leader. Creativity comes once a player is running with it. The players must realize that when they score, it is a team effort and not theirs alone. Many a football player has become lifted up in pride, thinking he alone was the reason his team won, but he must remember that the linemen cleared the way so he could score. If these linemen are unable to do their job, gifted athletes may be stopped on the scrimmage line.

In our analogy, the linemen represent the office staff and ministry of helps. Associate ministers depend on these people to clear obstacles out of the way, so their gifts can come forth. The associates must never lose sight of this fact. Every position on the staff is necessary to the ministry's success.

Developing the Spirit of an Armorbearer

- What is your position on the team? Who fills each of the other positions?

- Make it a point today to let the other team members know that you appreciate all they do to make the team function smoothly.

- If any of your other teammates seem not to fit their position, pray for God to move them into the proper place. God's best is for each person to find the position he was created to fill.

Father, thank You for making me part of this team. I pray that each of us would fill the position that is best suited for us, and I trust You to make any necessary adjustments. Thank You for the Holy Spirit who communicates each move to our leader, who in turn communicates it to us. Help each of us carry out the duties

341

of our positions well, so we can move the vision forward to its intended goal. Amen.

THE LINEMEN

Those parts of the body that seem to be weaker are indispensable, and the parts that we think are less honorable we treat with special honor. And the parts that are unpresentable are treated with special modesty, while our presentable parts need no special treatment. But God has combined the members of the body and has given greater honor to the parts that lacked it, so that there should be no division in the body, but that its parts should have equal concern for each other. If one part suffers, every part suffers with it; if one part is honored, every part rejoices with it (1 Corinthians 12:22-26 NIV).

In studying a football team to help us understand the structure for ministry leaders and their staffs, the linemen are the backbone and workhorses of the offense. Their job is to protect the quarterback and clear the way for the backs and ends to gain yardage. The linemen must listen to each play called and for the snap count, even if they are tired or hurt. They must have a great tolerance for pain.

Linemen do not get a lot of fanfare; nevertheless, they experience great joy when their team scores. They are always the toughest and strongest on the team and must be determined that no defensive lineman is going to get through. Their attitude is that no one sacks their quarterback or catches their backs behind the line.

The linemen are the equivalent to the office staff and ministry of helps. They are the backbone of a church or ministry. They must stay built up, have a winning attitude, and be determined that no devil will get to their leader. They do not receive most of the fanfare, but every ministry leader and associate knows they can do nothing without these workers. Victory would not be possible without them.

The linemen must listen carefully to the leader to know the direction in which the team is going. Their greatest joy comes when souls are born into the Kingdom of God and people are set free, in part because they did their jobs.

Teams win through unity, motivation for winning, determination, endurance, practice, and ability. These are all true in the ministry as well. When one scores, all score. When one wins, the whole team wins. At the end of the Super Bowl, all the players on the winning team receive special rings and a big bonus check. No matter their position, each player receives the same prizes. As we are faithful to our positions, we—like Super Bowl champs—will receive from

God the same reward because we did the job He called us to do and we won as a team.

Developing the Spirit of an Armorbearer

- Whether you are a "lineman" or hold another position on your team, make it a special point to bless these indispensable members. Often overlooked, a pat on the back for a job well done may be just the word of encouragement that fellow workers need. Make their day.

- The following are verses for study and meditation:

"Finally, all of you, live in harmony with one another; be sympathetic, love as brothers, be compassionate and humble. Do not repay evil with evil or insult with insult, but with blessing, because to this you were called so that you may inherit a blessing" (1 Peter 3:8-9 NIV).

"Only let your conversation be as it becometh the gospel of Christ: that whether I come and see you, or else be absent, I may hear of your affairs, that ye stand fast in one spirit, with one mind striving together for the faith of the gospel" (Philippians 1:27).

Father God, Your unconditional love is amazing. Only You would have such a creative way of making all of Your children feel significant—because they are! Help

me to appreciate the place You've designated for me in the Body as well as the placement of the other believers with whom I come into contact. Help us to support, encourage, and assist one another in a spirit of unity, so that together we can accomplish the vision You have given our leader. Amen.

WALKING WITHOUT OFFENSE

If it is possible, as much as depends on you, live peaceably with all men (Romans 12:18).

Another key to teamwork that is a must in fulfilling the vision of a ministry is to walk without offense. The main reason people leave churches and ministries is because they get offended. Instead of dealing with whatever was said or done, they harbor bitterness and end up leaving.

I saw a documentary on TV once that showed how Africans catch monkeys. First, some men put a cage on the ground with a bright object inside it. The door to the cage was left open to tempt the monkey to go in. It was constructed so that when the monkey would go in, a trap was set on the door to cause it to close and catch him. But the monkey would not go into the cage.

So the Africans closed the cage. Then they adjusted the wire around the cage so that the space in between the wires was just big enough for the monkey to get his hand into the cage. Then, when the monkey saw the bright object, he put his hand through one of the openings and grabbed the thing—but he couldn't get it out of the cage. With the object in hand, he could not pull it through. The only thing that would free him was to let go of the object, which he refused to do.

Then one of the Africans took a club and knocked the monkey over the head, and it died. Many who are backslidden today are like that monkey. They reached into the devil's "cage" by taking hold of an offense and have refused to let go. The devil is hitting them over the head with sickness, strife, and all types of marriage, family, and financial problems. They have given themselves over to bitterness, and it is destroying them.

All they have to do to be free and remain free is to *let go* of hurts and wounds. God can heal and restore a person immediately if he will forgive offenses and repent of bitterness.

Some readers have been hurt by ministry leaders or their staffs and have allowed resentment to build up. If you are resigning from the ministry you work for or you are leaving your church, *please stop!* Go to the person who has offended you, and ask him to forgive you. Talk with him about the situation. Perhaps you have misunderstood something. Perhaps sharing your point of view might help. If you disagree, you can disagree without being disagreeable or offended.

The bottom line is not to allow any offense to come between you and any other person. This is the only way you are going to have true peace in your heart and family.

Anyone can take offense, get hurt, and walk out, but it takes a real man or woman of God to make it right. A true armorbearer always seeks reconciliation and forgiveness. Do it and be free.

Developing the Spirit of an Armorbearer

Meditate on the following Scriptures today, then act on them.

- *"Pursue peace with all people, and holiness, without which no one will see the Lord: looking carefully lest anyone fall short of the grace of God; lest any root of bitterness springing up cause trouble, and by this many become defiled"* (Hebrews 12:14-15).

- *"Therefore, as God's chosen people, holy and dearly loved, clothe yourselves with compassion, kindness, humility, gentleness, and patience. Bear with each other and forgive whatever grievances you may have against one another. Forgive as the Lord forgave you"* (Colossians 3:12-13 NIV).

Heavenly Father, I am really hurt. The last thing I want to do is ask for forgiveness. I know I can't retaliate, and everything in me wants to flee. But that is not

Your way. I refuse to allow bitterness to take root in me, and I choose to walk in love. I will humble myself and go to this individual to seek forgiveness and reconciliation. I pray that You will be involved in our communication, and I am believing You to heal, restore, and bless. Amen.

USING ALL YOUR
TALENTS & ABILITIES

For the kingdom of heaven is as a man travelling into a far country, who called his own servants, and delivered unto them his goods. And unto one he gave five talents, to another two, and to another one; to every man according to his several ability and straightway took his journey (Matthew 25:14-15).

Using all your talents and abilities is another important key to teamwork. The Church must function like a team, and in order to do so, the team needs your talents and abilities.

In the parable of the talents, Jesus compares the Kingdom of God to a man taking a far journey and calling his servants together. This reveals Jesus as the One taking the journey, and He has called you and me together and has delivered unto us His goods. Each of us has received something from Him.

Jesus used money as the example, but in verse 35 continued, *"For I was an hungered, and ye gave me meat: I was thirsty and ye gave me drink."*

Jesus gave to one five talents and to another two talents and to another one. This proves to us that He was not only referring to money, but also to our using the gifts and callings we have been given to help others. So I am going to use the word "talents" to refer to our gifts and callings. Like the man in the parable, Jesus then took His journey, only His journey took place after He was raised from the dead. Now He has given to each of us certain talents to be used for His Kingdom.

You may say, "Brother Nance, I don't have any gifts or talents."

But you do, according to First Peter 4:10 (NASB), which says, *"As each one has received a special gift, employ it in serving one another as good stewards of the manifold grace of God."* Your talents may just be lying dormant, waiting to be used.

In the midst of being faithful where God has placed you, by faith begin to draw on the abilities within you. You have the Creator on the inside. Pray and trust Him for His complete will to be fulfilled in your life. You will be blessed, as will everyone else in your world.

Developing the Spirit of an Armorbearer

- If you are not clear as to what gifts and talents you possess, think about those things you are good at, strengths that others have commented on. What brings you the greatest joy in life? Maybe you love talking to people. Maybe you're a detail person. Perhaps you are task oriented. These are all indicators to consider when trying to recognize the gifts God has endowed you with.

- If you already know your talents and are flowing in them, purposely think of them as a gift you can give others—or better yet, a gift that God wants to give others through you.

- The following are some verses for study and meditation:

"It is the one and only Holy Spirit who distributes these gifts. He alone decides which gift each person should have" (1 Corinthians 12:11 NLT).

"For the gifts and calling of God are without repentance" (Romans 11:29).

"A man's gift maketh room for him, and bringeth him before great men" (Proverbs 18:15).

Father God, thank You for the gifts and callings You have given me. I want to develop them to their highest potential. If there are some I am not aware of, I ask You to reveal them to me. By faith I draw on these precious

resources for the good of those I come into contact with and the ministry I serve. Amen.

YOU'RE ONLY RESPONSIBLE
FOR THE GIFTS YOU'VE BEEN GIVEN

Make a careful exploration of who you are and the work you have been given, and then sink yourself into that. Don't be impressed with yourself. Don't compare yourself with others. Each of you must take responsibility for doing the creative best you can with your own life (Galatians 6:3-5 TM).

We have no choice in the matter; Jesus is the One who gave out the talents that we possess. So if you have two talents and someone else has five, it does no good to be jealous or complain.

God did not call me to His throne before I was born and say, "Terry, I am now ready to allow you to be born in the earth, but before you go, which gifts would you like to take with you?"

If He had, I would have said, "Well, Lord! Give me the gift of the apostle and that gift of the prophet; and while

You're at it, throw in the gifts of healing and working of miracles."

The bottom line is that each of us is only accountable for our own gifts and callings and not for someone else's. Matthew 25:19 tells us there will come a "reckoning day." Romans 14:10 says that we will all stand before the judgment seat of Christ.

I know personally, I will not stand before God and give account to Him for the ability to play the drums. I cannot play the drums, because I have very little rhythm. If it's not there, it's not there. But I do have other abilities, which I can use to bless the Kingdom of God.

In the parable of the talents in Matthew 25, notice in verses 22 and 23 that Jesus said to the one who had received two talents the same thing He said to the first one to whom He gave five talents. This proves to us that if we are faithful to do what God has given us to do, we will receive the same rewards. God only holds you responsible for what He has given you. If you are faithful to do that and the leader you serve is faithful to do what God has called him to do, then you will both receive the same reward.

The Spirit of God is saying loud and clear that it is time for us to release our gifts. We do not want to be like the servant in the parable who received one talent and simply buried it. That man was called a "wicked and slothful servant." On the other hand, do not be like the man who prayed, "God, use me! Use me!" then, after working in the ministry for a while, went back to the Lord and said, "Lord, I feel used."

What God has called you to do is significant, and no one can flow in that gift quite like you can. Be faithful with it to the glory of God.

Developing the Spirit of an Armorbearer

- In what ways are you putting your gifts to work?

- Do you have some talents that are not being put to use? What can you do to change that?

- In what ways have you observed your gifts blessing others?

Heavenly Father, when I meet You face to face, I want to hear You say, "Well done, good and faithful servant." I am committed to fulfilling my responsibility where my gifts and talents are concerned. I don't ever want to take them for granted or let them lie dormant. Thank You for using me to touch others. Amen.

RUN WITH THE VISION

And the multitude of them that believed were of one heart and of one soul (Acts 4:32).

In Acts 4, we are told of the disciples being threatened for praying in Jesus' name. They came together with the brethren and began to pray, and when they had prayed, the house where they were was shaken. They were all filled with the Holy Spirit and spoke God's Word with boldness. (v. 31.)

Our text makes a very important point. The "multitude of them that believed" were all of *"one heart and one soul."* In other words, they were in agreement. That is the key to seeing a great shaking of the Holy Spirit in our churches, cities, and ministries. We are all of one heart when we are born again, because we all belong to Jesus. But are we all "one soul"?

A corporate anointing came on the believers in our text, because they were in unity. They all had the same vision— to take the Gospel to the world no matter the personal cost. They were determined to flow together, to recognize the authority of the apostles, and to follow what Jesus was saying through them.

God speaks the vision into the heart of a local pastor or a ministry leader, and that vision must get inside the believers. Then they are to run with their heart and soul toward the fulfillment of it. In the case of a local church, a corporate anointing will impact a city.

What is the vision of your pastor for the local church? Or if you work for a ministry, what is the vision of your leader? Take hold of that vision and begin to run with it, heart and soul. One way that we can do this is to "all speak the same thing" and have no divisions among us, as Paul exhorted the Corinthians (1 Corinthians 1:10).

If you are trying to run with a vision that God has not given your leader, then you are going to create division. You need to stop and hook up with what God is saying to him and begin running in the same direction.

Do you really want to do exploits for God? Are you willing to find your place in the Body and get connected with the other members? Are you ready to release the gifts and talents God has put in you? If so, begin by becoming involved. God will never force Himself on you. He gives you the right to choose. But think of what can be accomplished for God's Kingdom when you begin to do your part!

We are called to be armorbearers one for another. That commitment is a lifetime responsibility. Now is the time to pick up your spiritual sword and join the ranks of God's great army. We will stand victorious together because where one will put a thousand to flight, two will put ten thousand to flight (Leviticus 26:8).

Developing the Spirit of an Armorbearer

- What is the condition of your local church or the ministry you are associated with? Is there unity, oneness of heart and soul? Is everyone speaking the same thing? If not, repent of any part you may have played in spreading division and strife. Also, pray for any others who may not be hooked up heart and soul.

- Consider the following about those who constructed the Tower of Babel: *"And the Lord said, Behold, the people is one, and they have all one language; and this they begin to do: and now nothing will be restrained from them, which they have imagined to do"* (Gen. 11:6). If such agreement can work in the negative, think of how we in the Body of Christ can put this principle to work!

Heavenly Father, I long for the corporate anointing that the disciples experienced. I will be faithful to follow my leader's vision, and I vow never to take off in another direction. I will not allow myself to be involved in any

division or strife but will hook up with my leader, heart and soul. Thank You for accomplishing exploits through us. Amen.

PRAYER OF SALVATION

God loves you—no matter who you are, no matter what your past. God loves you so much that He gave His one and only begotten Son for you. The Bible tells us that "...whoever believes in him shall not perish but have eternal life" (John 3:16 NIV). Jesus laid down His life and rose again so that we could spend eternity with Him in Heaven and experience His absolute best on earth. If you would like to receive Jesus into your life, say the following prayer out loud and mean it from your heart.

Heavenly Father, I come to You admitting that I am a sinner. Right now, I choose to turn away from sin, and I ask You to cleanse me of all unrighteousness. I believe that Your Son, Jesus, died on the Cross to take away my sins. I also believe that He rose again from the dead so that I might be forgiven of my sins and made righteous through faith in Him. I call upon the name of Jesus Christ to be the Savior and Lord of my life. Jesus, I choose to follow You and ask that You fill me with the power of the Holy Spirit. I declare that right now I am

363

a child of God. I am free from sin and full of the righteousness of God. I am saved in Jesus' name. Amen.

ABOUT THE AUTHOR

TERRY NANCE is the founder and president of Focus on the Harvest, Inc. Terry received a personal mandate from the Lord and has committed his life's calling to travel to local congregations throughout the nations and awaken believers to this strategic generation. Through his God-given passion, believers are ignited to discover their individual gifts and callings, commit to the vision of their local church, and focus on the harvest of souls throughout their city, state, nation, and world.

A graduate of Southwestern Assemblies of God Bible College and Rhema Bible Training Center, Terry formerly served over 23 years as the senior associate and executive director of the Agape School of World Evangelism and Agape Missionary Alliance under the leadership of Happy Caldwell and Agape Church in Little Rock, Arkansas. He was also the executive director of the Agape Belize International Training Center in Central America. Reproducing a spirit of excellence in integrity, the graduating students under Terry's leadership continue to revolutionize the nations for God by raising up schools and churches in nations such as Belize, England, Mexico, the Philippines, Sweden, Finland, Romania, Norway, Iceland, India, Scotland, and Niger.

Terry has authored three books: *God's Armorbearer I—How To Serve God's Leaders; God's Armorbearer II—Bloom Where You are Planted;* and *Vision of the House—Charting Your Course to Destiny.* On the bestselling list for the past ten years, these books have motivated thousands of Christians to stand with their leaders in faithful service, helping to fulfill God's vision for the nations.

To contact Terry Nance for speaking engagements
or for information on materials, please write,
call,or visit the Web site at:

FOCUS ON THE HARVEST, INC.
P.O. Box 7087
Springdale, AR 72766
479-872-0777

www.godsarmorbearer.com
tnance@focusontheharvest.com

Please include your prayer requests and comments
when you write.

OTHER BOOKS BY TERRY NANCE

God's Armorbearer Volumes I and II—Revised

God's Armorbearer Study Guide

Vision of the House

ADDITIONAL COPIES OF THIS BOOK ARE AVAILABLE
FROM YOUR LOCAL BOOKSTORE.

Additional copies of this book and other
book titles from DESTINY IMAGE are
available at your local bookstore.

Call toll-free: 1-800-722-6774

Send a request for a catalog to:

Destiny Image® Publishers, Inc.
P.O. Box 310
Shippensburg, PA 17257-0310

*"Speaking to the Purposes of God for This
Generation and for the Generations to Come."*

**For a complete list of our titles,
visit us at www.destinyimage.com**